Whoops, there goes another Tree Plant! *Ray Villie*

Keep High Hopes, *Larry Pears*

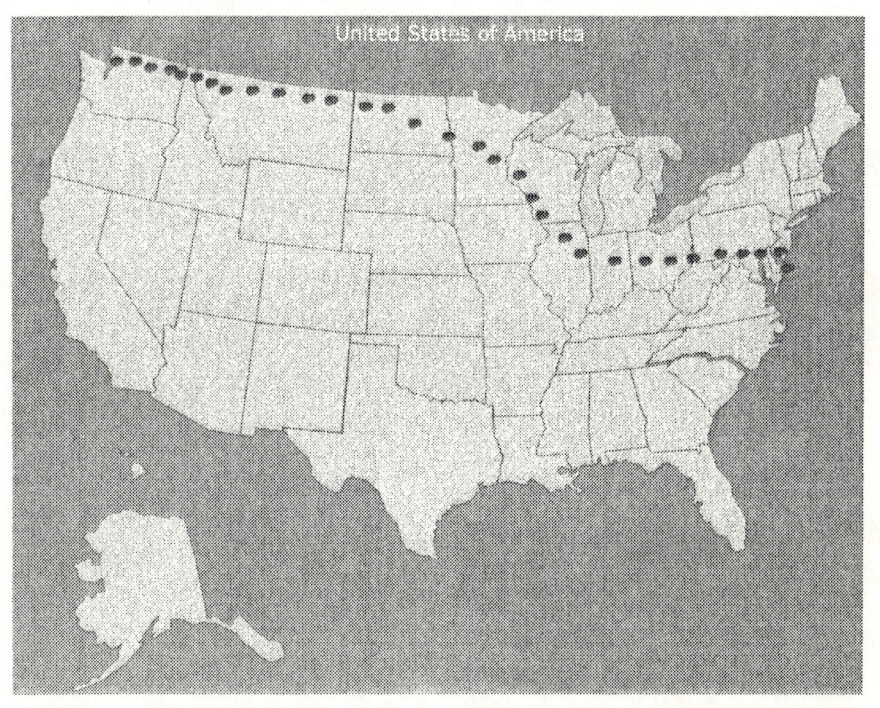

One Pedal at a time
J. P. Budd

"One day at a time"
Kim O'Neal

High Hopes

Rob Sorantino

Bloomington, IN  Milton Keynes, UK

AuthorHouse™
1663 Liberty Drive, Suite 200
Bloomington, IN 47403
www.authorhouse.com
Phone: 1-800-839-8640

AuthorHouse™ UK Ltd.
500 Avebury Boulevard
Central Milton Keynes, MK9 2BE
www.authorhouse.co.uk
Phone: 08001974150

© *2006 Rob Sorantino. All rights reserved.*

No part of this book may be reproduced, stored in a retrieval system, or transmitted by any means without the written permission of the author.

First published by AuthorHouse 7/5/2006

ISBN: 1-4259-3304-1 (sc)

Printed in the United States of America
Bloomington, Indiana

This book is printed on acid-free paper.

Dedication

I dedicate this book to my daughters, Anna and Lauren, who help me to realize every day what is really important in life. Thank you for just being the way you are.

This book is also dedicated to cancer patients everywhere who fight valiantly each day.

Acknowledgment

I would like to acknowledge my wife for supporting me in going on this trip and taking care of everything while I was gone. She has always been supportive of anything I aspired to do in life.

This book would not have been possible without my traveling companions: J.P., Ray, Larry, Tim, Elaine, Mary Ann, Cynthia, and Pat. I want to thank them for their help and support during our ride and with this book.

Introduction

Before I left for the trip, I knew it would be important for me to capture the experience by keeping a log. After the long, challenging days of riding, I wrote in the log each night. I was so tired that at times I woke up in the middle of the night with the log on my stomach and the pen still in my hand with partially written sentences.

I'm glad I kept the log. There was so much happening each day that it would be impossible to retain it all. We were on bicycles riding along a rural route 3,400 miles across the country determined to make it in 31 days. It was an experience like no other I've ever had or may ever have again.

I thought there was a possibility, late in life, I would write about my experiences for future generations. I never thought I'd have anything noteworthy enough occur in my life (and hoped I didn't have anything tragic enough) to write about in a book. But when we reached the Atlantic after 3,400 miles and 31 consecutive days of riding, I knew using the log to write a book would make the journey seem more real to me and help capture the many experiences for a lifetime.

You'll see that these chapters are very short and the book is a quick read. The purpose of the book is two fold – for you to take the journey with us and to raise money for a worthy cause. Although we raised nearly $44,000 for the Helen F. Graham Cancer Center, 50% of the profit from this book will also be donated to the cancer center. I hope you enjoy it!

Biographies of the Riders

John Patrick Budd: J.P., 28 years old at the time of the ride, was born in Brooklyn, N.Y., but grew up in Delaware. He is a graduate of the University of North Carolina at Wilmington and a former Marine. In 2003, J.P.'s father developed terminal cancer. The idea to travel from coast to coast on a bicycle was a goal of his since he graduated from college. While stationed overseas in the Marine Corps, he thought of ways in which he could help his and other families in their struggle to beat cancer.

Tim O'Neill: Tim, 62 years old at the time of the ride, was diagnosed with an advanced stage of cancer in 1992. He underwent chemotherapy, massive radiation, and surgery. To help him regain his strength, Tim set the goal of hiking with his family up the Glaciers of Mount Rainier in Washington. After doing this, Tim decided to backpack the Appalachian Trail to continue his recovery. He did it in sections over eight years. Last year, his daughter-in-law was diagnosed with terminal cancer and died only a month prior to his coast-to-coast ride. His long struggle with cancer made him want to do something to help others, and he continues to be involved in various cancer causes.

Larry Peart: Larry, 66 years old at the time of the ride, is a native of Wilmington, Del., and a graduate of Salesianum High School and the University of Delaware. He and his wife, Mary Ann, have a son, Patrick; a daughter, Erin; and three grandchildren. Larry's mother died of cancer at age 52. He began cycling with Ray and Tim in 2001. Larry and Mary Ann, both cycling enthusiasts, are members of the White Clay Bicycle Club and the Sussex Cyclists.

Rob Sorantino: Rob, 41 years old at the time of the ride, grew up in New Jersey, then moved to Delaware as a teenager. He is a graduate of the University of Delaware. He and his wife, Terri, have two daughters, Anna and Lauren. Rob stays physically active exercising each day and periodically participating in triathlons and swim meets. He took up biking at age 40 when he decided to try completing a triathlon.

Ray Villec: Ray, 64 years old at the time of the ride, was born and raised in New Jersey. He and his wife, Cynthia, moved to Delaware in 1976. They have two sons and three grandchildren. Ray began riding in 1977 to strengthen his knee and hasn't stopped since. He is an avid member of the White Clay Bicycle Club, and this was his second cross-country bike trip— having ridden almost 4,000 miles in a month on the last trek when he was 41.

Chapter I
Background

From my earliest memories of what I wanted my life to be about and what I wanted to experience, I can tell you that riding a bike across the United States at 41 years of age was not anywhere on my radar screen. I also didn't think in terms of combining such an effort with a fundraising and awareness campaign that could have an impact on so many people's lives. But this ride, as I will share with you in these pages, ended up being one of the most important experiences in my life so far. No matter what I've accomplished or will accomplish in life, the ride will always be one of my most significant accomplishments. It helped me get my feet firmly planted at a time when I really needed it.

How did it all start? Well, let me take you back to March of 2004, shortly after I turned 40. A couple of friends had participated in a triathlon, and listening to them talk about the experience sparked my interest in doing one too. My main sports when I was a kid were swimming and running, and I felt pretty confident in my ability to train for and handle those legs of the race. But I had never really done any biking, especially since I was in a serious bike accident when I was 10 years old. My father-in-law gave me the Cannondale road bike he bought in 1986, and I had it tuned up. The bike more than served my needs to pursue the training I needed for the triathlon. Toward the end of my very first ride on the bike, a group of cyclists rode up next to me and one of them asked with whom I rode. "Nobody," I said. The cyclist invited me to ride with the group and gave me his e-mail address to use if I were interested in meeting them the next weekend. I committed it to memory and went home and e-mailed him my name and phone number. He contacted me later that week and gave me a time and place to meet that coming Saturday morning. Little did I know that my e-mailing Tim O'Neill would open the gate to a new and exciting chapter of my life.

I showed up at the designated meeting place on Saturday morning and rode with the group. They were very friendly, and before long I recognized that this arrangement was going to continue at some level even after the triathlon took place. The members of the group had a simple, friendly camaraderie, and they quickly made me a part of it. They were all significantly older than me, and I enjoyed watching them joke around and interacting with them. We formed a unique bond, and I was happily surprised to see how important they would be in helping me get through a few common midlife issues. It's clear to me now how valuable a group of friends like these can be. They had walked in the shoes I was currently wearing, and their wisdom and guidance about how they handled life's ups and downs and the eventual outcomes were incredibly helpful to me. Some of these guys became more like mentors than friends. Their wisdom came into my life not a minute too soon.

Chapter II

The idea to ride across the United States

Our routine was to ride on Saturday and Sunday mornings. We never rode more than 25 miles, and I thought those were long rides. Little did I know that I would agree to and actually ride a bicycle 3,400 miles from the Pacific to the Atlantic in 31 days. If you had told me that was in the cards for me, I would have confidently told you that you were talking about someone else. Besides, how does a 41-year-old corporate guy with a wife and two daughters, aged 8 and 11, drop out of his life and go away on a bike trip for 31 days? Well, the stars aligned, and it happened.

I'll tell you about those stars and how they aligned. First, among Ray Villec's neighbors were the Budds. J.P. Budd, who was on a five-year tour as a U.S. Marine until August 2005, found out late in 2004 that his father was terminally ill with lung cancer. One of J.P.'s life goals was to ride a bicycle across the United States, so he decided to combine that goal with a fundraiser for cancer research and call it "Coast to Coast to Cure Cancer" to benefit the Helen F. Graham Cancer Center in Newark, Del. I found out about this ride in January 2005. While I knew very few details, it sounded so exciting that I said I wanted to go half the way because I felt comfortable that I could get away for two weeks, to participate for that long. The midpoint was Fargo, N.D., and I planned to get a Greyhound bus home from there and see the rest of the country through a bus window. Ray, who was 64 years old, had known J. P. Budd since J.P. was two years old. I had never met J.P. until a couple of weeks before the ride when he came home after completing his tour of duty. We quickly became friends.

I worked with J.P. as time allowed in the weeks prior to the ride to help get things organized and to promote the ride to generate contributions. One of the things I did was get in touch with the communications people at the company where I worked, and they did a story on the ride and the cause. The story generated a lot of awareness, and the donations started to roll in. A great many people at the company were always ready to contribute their time and/or money to worthwhile causes. In the days following the article, several people I worked with approached me and asked why I was only riding halfway. I explained that I didn't think of requesting, or taking off, a month, even though I had enough vacation time.

Also, about a month before the ride, the company announced that it was being purchased. Based on the types of projects I was working on, the brakes were put on my assignments until the acquiring company decided on the next steps. Shortly after this announcement it became apparent that my job was at risk, due to duplication. The consistent message I received from people all around was that it was all right to request the time off, given the climate of the work environment, and that I would probably never have an opportunity to do anything like this again.

Planning the trip on paper, I found I had just enough vacation days to make the whole trip, as long as there were no delays. My manager was glad to approve the vacation time.

Now the fear began. In the days following, I began to prepare for what I was going to experience. At first I was excited. Then I became scared—scared of the unknown, and scared about whether I could actually pull it off. I asked myself, "What if I can't make it the whole way? What if I'm injured along the way?" Luckily, that fear turned into determination and excitement only a couple of days prior to leaving.

(Ray, J.P., Rob and Larry)

Chapter III

Leaving for the trip

With the exception of Tim who drove to Anacortes, WA on his own, the rest of us met at the Villec's house at 5:30 a.m. for breakfast. Much to my surprise, we made the front page of the local paper, the *News Journal*, and received almost a full-page spread on the second page of the paper. The *News Journal* did a great job of explaining our mission and getting it the attention it needed. The article included a piece on each rider and why the ride was important to him. I liked my wife's comment: "Wow! You made the front page of the paper and you didn't do anything wrong!" Mike Chalmers, the *News Journal* reporter, was practically a part of our group throughout the ride, and he did an outstanding job handling our story from beginning to end.

We all wore the bike jerseys donated to us by W.L. Gore, the manufacturers of Gore Bike Wear, on the plane ride to Seattle. As you can imagine, everyone on the plane was asking why we were dressed alike. As we explained what we were doing, we began to get a feel for how we were going to be received by the public throughout the trip. When the Southwest Air flight attendants came to understand our mission, they made a fuss over us. During the flight, one of them announced us as special guests on the plane and sang the song "High Hopes." We all know this song; it's the one that goes, "Just what makes that little old ant think he can move that rubber tree plant. Anyone knows an ant can't move a rubber tree plant; but he's got high hopes, he's got high hopes, he's got high apple pie in the sky hopes …" People joined in singing and it raised our spirits even higher. After the flight, the attendants insisted on getting a group shot with us. They were a blast. I'll make it a point to fly Southwest whenever I can.

After a layover in Phoenix, we flew to Seattle and took a shuttle to Anacortes, Wash. It was a long day, coming from the East Coast. We lost three hours with the time zone change and still arrived late in the day. We took our bikes out of the boxes and put them together, then went to dinner. Ray and I took a bike ride down by the water that evening before we turned in. While I rode, I thought about what we were about to do and felt a whole range of emotions. Regardless of how I felt, it was "game time," and suddenly everything else that seemed to weigh heavily in my life became less important. A single-minded focus was necessary to accomplish this goal, and I was inspired.

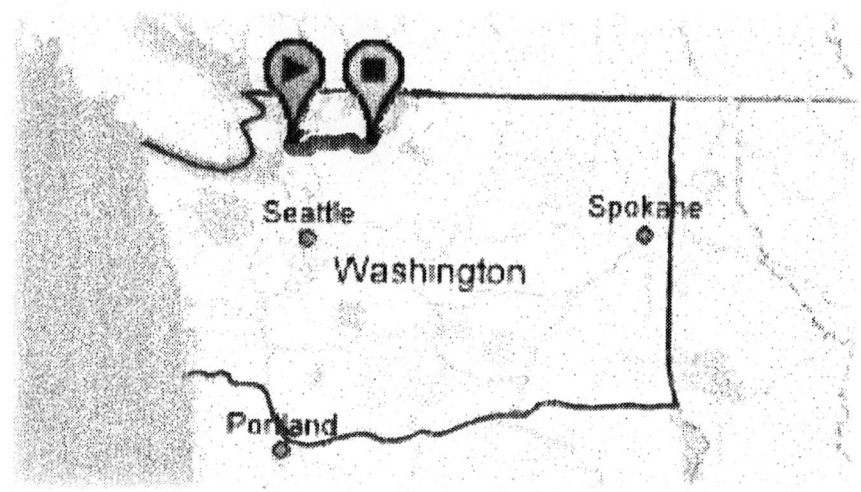

Day 1

8/14 -Washington

"This 100-mile-a-day stuff is harder than I thought it was going to be."

The next morning, a photographer sent by the *News Journal* showed up and took a lot of pictures, including us dipping our bike wheels in the Pacific. Technically, the body of water was Samish Bay, near Puget Sound off the Pacific Ocean, but we counted it as the Pacific. The weather was fantastic. Little did we know that the weather would be fantastic throughout the trip.

Keeping in mind that I had never ridden more than 65 miles in one bike ride and had exceeded 40 miles only three times, we set out for our first day. Huge mountains off in the distance came closer, and as the day progressed we started to see snow-capped mountains. We rode through small towns that did a great job letting you know you had entered the town with large signs indicating what the town was known for. One of the first notable towns was called Sedro-Wooley, Wash.

Washington is known for its evergreens, and they were everywhere. As we climbed to higher elevations, the mountains were covered with them. Needless to say everything looked very different from Delaware. Just before we reached Skagit Valley, we stopped at a restaurant for lunch. Our ride that day ended in a little town called Marblemount, Wash. We ate at the World Famous Buffalo Inn and stayed at the hotel by the same name. And yes, we did eat buffalo burgers for dinner. To give you an idea how small the town is, the Buffalo Inn was the only restaurant and hotel in town. And though the town was only about a city block long, it did have two gas stations. This was our destination for the day because the next lodgings were about 70 miles beyond Marblemount on the other side of the Washington Pass.

The mountains around this small town were enormous, and there were some beautiful creeks in the area—crystal blue with big, colorful river rocks at the bottom. I saw some good-sized fish jumping to eat bugs off the top of the water. That evening, after 45 miles of riding, I commented, "This 100-mile-a-day stuff is going to be harder than I thought it was going to be." The guys laughed, but they reminded me of that comment for the entire trip.

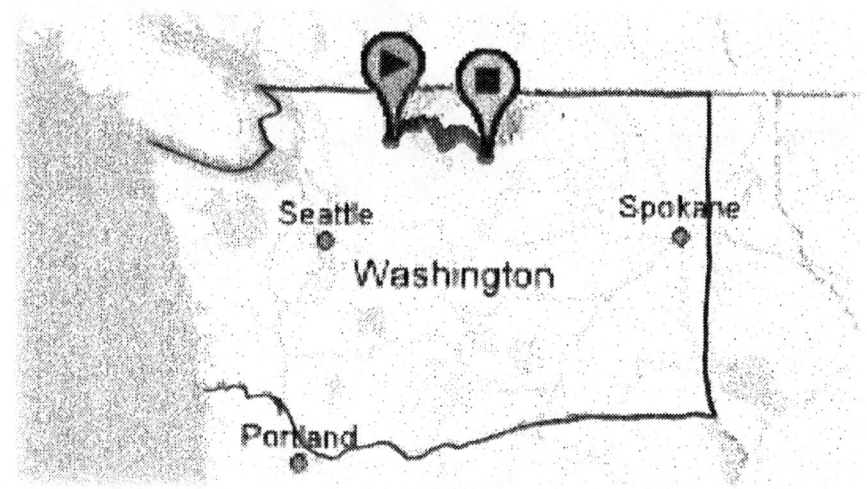

Day 2
8/15 - Washington
A lesson regarding dehydration

Without exception, everyone we talked to who had been over the Washington Pass raved about how beautiful it was. We found that Seattle City Light, the local power supplier, has a few dams in the area, and we also went through a couple of tunnels. We were stopped by flaggers early on because there is quite a lot of dynamiting in the area. Between the trucks carrying boulders and the logging trucks, we had to ride carefully.

The Washington Pass over the Cascade Mountains was all it was built up to be—absolutely beautiful. At times, we seemed to be on a Hollywood set because it seemed so unreal. And the mountains were enormous. They really did something for your sense of scale, making large skyscrapers look minuscule.

The day was full of excitement. Ray was nauseous, apparently due to something he had eaten the day before; and I got dehydrated on the way to the top of the pass. My lack of biking experience was showing. I had to sit out for a half-hour and drink about enough water to make my molars float, but I did gain enough energy to continue.

The top was amazing. The peaks of the mountain were solid rock, some snow-capped with fewer evergreens. I would get used to riding down a mountain on a bike, but this was the first time. I was surprised at how dangerous it could be if you didn't stay aware and maintain control every second. I pumped the brakes, as I'd been told, to keep them from overheating. It was very scenic, but it was a long way down.

This was our first mountain; and, given the differences in our biking abilities, we became separated. We regrouped in a little western-style town called Winthrop, Wash. It looked like the kind of town where you could tie your horse to a hitching post or see a gunfight break out at any moment. After having some ice cream (I didn't yet realize that this would become an event that occurred several times daily), we rode to our day destination of Twisp, Wash. We found out at dinner that the word Twisp is a modification of the Native American word, "T-wapsp," which means "yellow jacket," and "Twistsp," which means "sound of the buzzing wasp."

We stayed at the Idle-A-While Motel and met some nice people at dinner. Our waitress told us that she had recently lost her father to cancer, and it was clear that her emotional wound was still fresh.

We began to see how warm and friendly people in this part of the country are. It had been a hard day of riding, but I was told that this was probably our hardest day of the trip. Yeah, right! As it turned out, the next day would punish us beyond belief.

Day 3
8/16 - Washington
"Groundhog Day"

The next day we had to cross two mountain passes and cover a little more than 100 miles. We rode through the Okanogan National Forest and then the Colville National Forest. Given that the day before was supposedly the hardest day of the trip, I didn't worry too much. The first mountain pass wasn't too bad; and, after coming down the other side, we stopped for a late breakfast/early lunch. We had already begun telling the people we met that our mission was to raise cancer awareness and the funds to support cancer research. Wearing the same bicycle jerseys everywhere we went helped a lot.

Our waitress took an immediate interest in our cause and shared hers with us. Her 23-month-old granddaughter was in the hospital with cancer, and doctors had recently removed one of her eyes due to her illness. We were beginning to realize that we would hear stories like this everywhere we went.

We rode about 40 miles and stopped for something to eat. Since we were burning so many calories each day, we found ourselves constantly eating. One of the good things about this trip was that I could eat anything I wanted and as much of it as I wanted, and it was all I could do to keep weight on. Anyone who knows me will know I was in seventh heaven. We stopped at a convenience store with booths where you could sit and eat. Unfortunately, no one took a picture, but the group of us, less J.P. who rode ahead, stretched our legs out and took a nap. Picture three men in their 60s and me, all dressed identically, four in a row, taking our afternoon naps! Larry was even using his windbreaker as a blanket. The picture would have been priceless. I slept so well I even had a dream. We were clearly loitering, and I have no idea how long we slept; but the people working there liked us because of our cause and didn't bother us.

We headed toward another mountain, and it was brutal to climb. Keep in mind that these mountain passes are about 15 to 20 miles on the way up and another 15 or 20 miles down the other side. You're doing well if you're able to maintain a pace of five miles an hour going up. It seemed to take forever to climb this mountain, and there were few signs of civilization along the way. To make matters worse, we were losing daylight, and we had no way of knowing how much farther the top of the mountain was.

Ray and I were so tired that we were walking our bikes at times. But Larry, the slowest member of our team and yet one of the most determined men you'd ever meet, was absolutely steady; and he passed us. As it began to get dark, we made it to the top of the mountain pass and began descending. That takes time too, because of the distance. The road also flattened out at times, and that took a lot of pedaling. I began to fear that the local wildlife would emerge. That was probably paranoia, but it had been an unbelievably hard day.

We made it to the bottom of the mountain and the entrance to Republic, Wash. just as it got dark. I was very glad to see civilization again. Even though four of us had to sleep in the same room, and J.P. and I had to sleep on the floor, I was glad to be there. Sleeping out on the mountain was not what I had in mind.

After almost 14 hours of riding that day, over two mountain passes and more than 100 miles, we ate pizza that night as though there were no tomorrow. You may remember the movie called *Groundhog Day*, starring Bill Murray and Andie McDowell, where Bill's character keeps waking up to the same day every day for an extended period. We joked that the ride was beginning to feel just like that.

Someone in town told me that Republic had been a gold rush town more than a hundred years ago, with more than 20,000 residents. Today it has only 600 residents.

Day 4

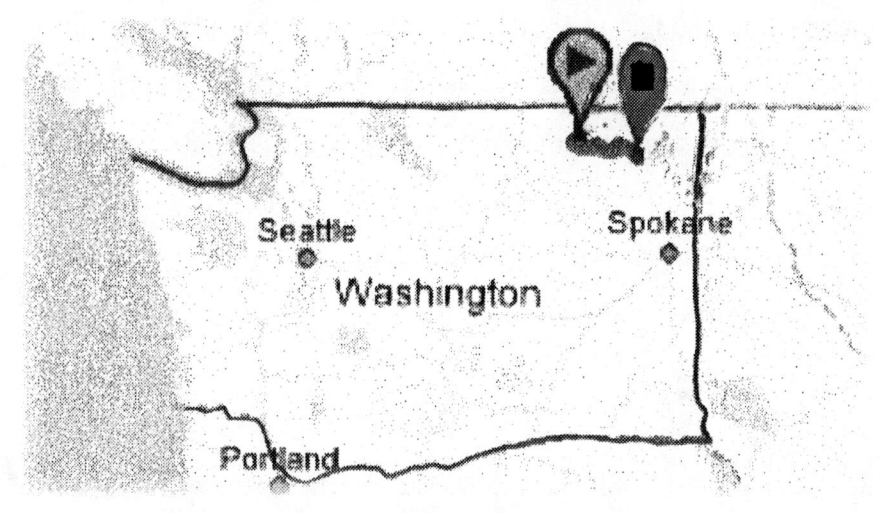

8/17 - Washington

Risk of hypothermia … in August?

After two difficult days in a row, I figured the next day had to be better. Unfortunately, it was challenging in its own right. We rode out of Republic and immediately began climbing Sherman Pass. We were still in the Colville National Forest and it was raining, but not hard. I didn't know that Sherman Pass was the highest pass in the state of Washington, and I'm not sure I would have cared if I had known prior to starting the day's ride.

I expected to be soaked when I got to the top, but I did not expect it to be 40 degrees. There was a thermometer indicating this at the peak, and now we were faced with going down the mountain soaking wet. Steam was coming off my body from sweat and cold. The support vehicle driven by Tim's wife, Elaine O'Neill, was waiting for us at the top. Luckily, Tim insisted I exchange my wind jacket and cycling jersey for dry garments. It was a good thing I did, because it was freezing going down the mountain. We all risked hypothermia, and Ray in particular was extremely cold. Even from a distance, I could see his body shaking while he was riding.

We stopped several times coming down the mountain to warm up, but it helped only a bit to get out of the wind and rain. When we got to the bottom, we went into a restaurant to warm up. We decided we would call it a day, even though we were 80 miles short of our objective.

Larry and I each had an Indian Taco for lunch, essentially a taco salad on something called fry bread. They were excellent. We stayed at a motel in Kettle Falls, Wash., near Lake Roosevelt. After the days we'd had, it was nice to have some time to relax and catch up.

We were only seven miles from the Canadian border. Lewis and Clark had stayed in this area on their expedition, and a nearby museum was rich in local history.

Believe it or not, two days after we left Kettle Falls, it snowed a couple of inches on Sherman Pass. Remember, it was mid-August.

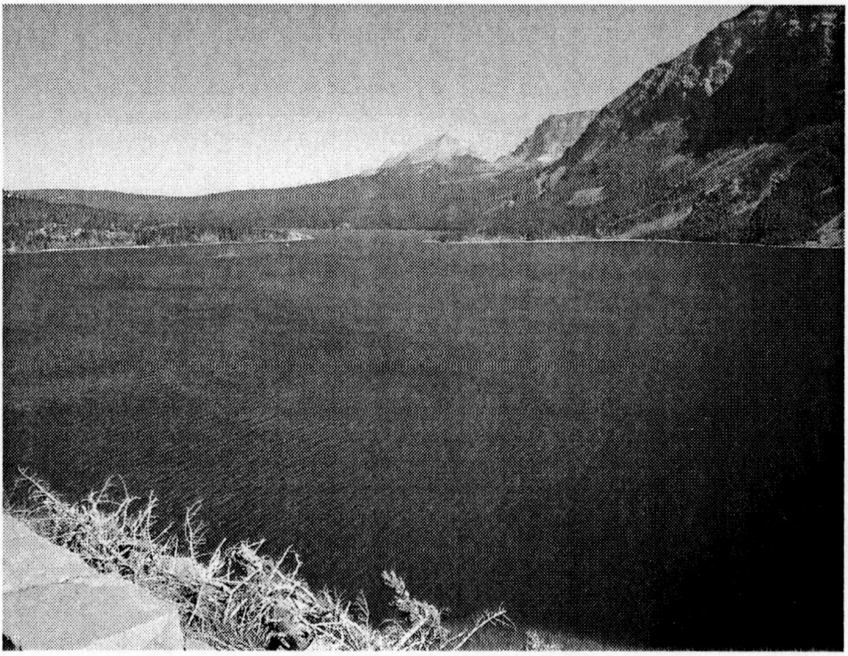

Day 5

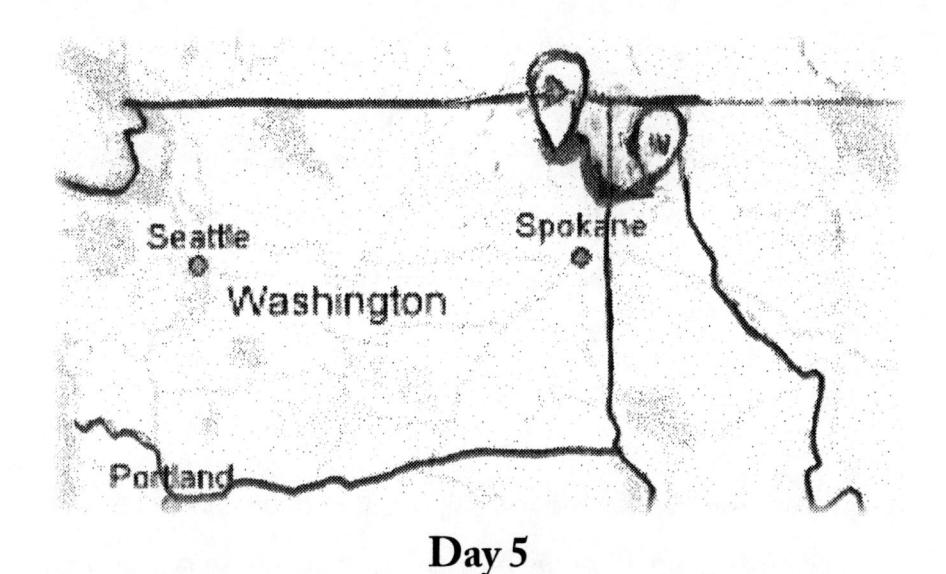

8/18 - Washington and Idaho

My first flat tire

The next morning we set out for Sandpoint, Idaho. We covered a total of 124 miles in 13 hours, and again it was a challenging day of riding. We were still in the Colville National Forest and passed into the Kaniksu National Forest later in the day. Early in the day we crossed Tiger Pass on the eastern side of Washington. I saw so many deer, I was concerned one might run out in my path. I also saw a flock of wild turkeys.

The biggest animal experience of the day was when a herd of cattle came out of the woods and crossed the road as we were going down Tiger Pass. That was scary. The cattle were huge, and they were running scared from something. We never figured out what it was, but we put as much distance as possible between them and us.

We rode along the Pend Orielle River most of the day, and the views were fantastic. Each part of Washington had slightly different mountain landscapes, and these were especially attractive. The combination of the mountains, the plush evergreens, the sky in three shades of blue, and the crystal-blue river was something to remember.

The temperature was in the high 60s for the day. We did something I felt was significant on this day of riding: We crossed into a new state. Idaho was absolutely beautiful. We had ridden on Route 20 for the entire trip up to this point, and it turned into Route 2 at the Idaho state line. As we traveled east on Route 2, we followed a wide river that snaked through a valley. Everywhere, mountains met the water. We were still riding close and parallel to the Canadian border, and Idaho is very narrow up in that portion of the state called "the panhandle." We also discovered that Idaho is known as the gem state.

It felt good to cross into a new state, but we didn't actually get to Sandpoint until dark. Tim and I were the last to arrive because I got my first flat tire about 10 miles from our final destination.

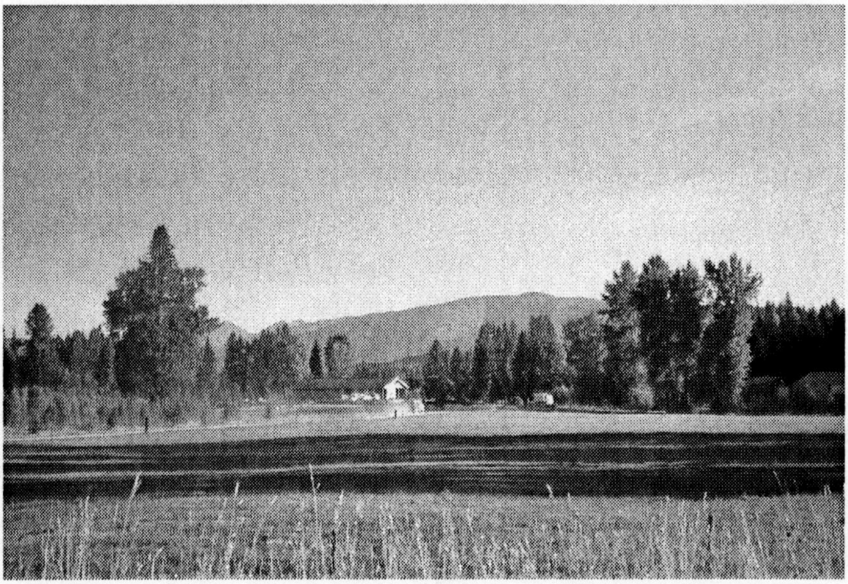

Day 6

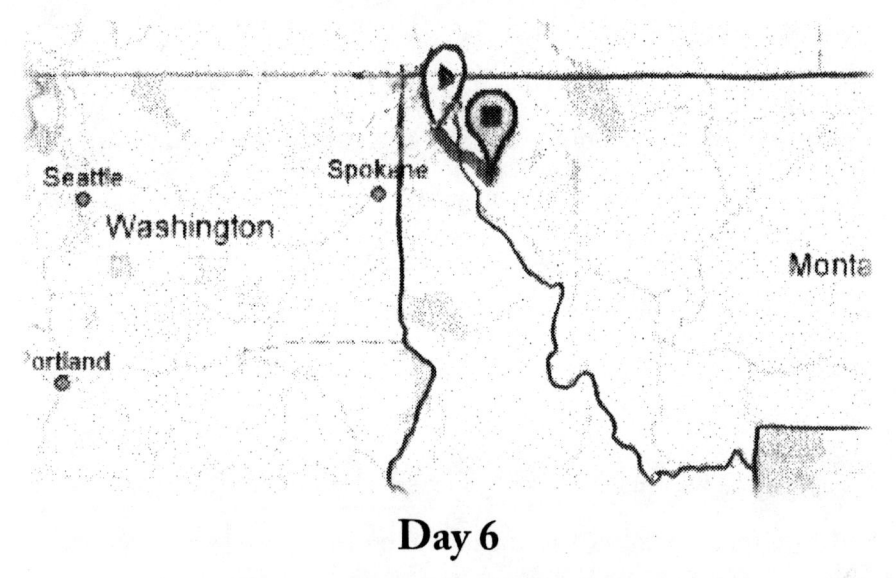

8/19 - Idaho and Montana
The Tascor Ranch

The next morning we set out for Trout Creek, Mont. When we got to Montana, we changed from Pacific Standard Time to Mountain Standard Time. The combination of getting to another new state so quickly, combined with the time change, did a lot for my morale, especially after the series of challenging days we had had. Fortunately, we had a short day of riding, only 74 miles; and we stayed with Ray's friend and her family on their ranch.

They enjoyed having us, and they were terrific hosts. Ray met Jeannie about 40 years ago when he lived in southern New Jersey, and he remembers when she and her husband, Lou, and Lou's brother Mark moved to Montana in the mid-70s. They live just outside Trout

Creek on a ranch consisting of several hundred acres, and Mark lives close by on a couple hundred acres of his own. They have happy hour almost daily on their porch, and it was just what we needed.

Lou and Mark were very handy. Their main business was trucking, but they had their hands in several different businesses. They had also built their own homes, which were stunning. To me, Lou and Mark are excellent examples of today's renaissance man. I'm sure that between them they could accomplish just about anything.

As usual, we ate like horses, then slept in the bunkhouse. Jeannie and Lou made breakfast for us in the morning, and they were very warm to us for the short time we were there. I was struck by how friendly all the members of their extended family were to one another. It was fantastic to see such good family relationships, and I was envious. I missed my family.

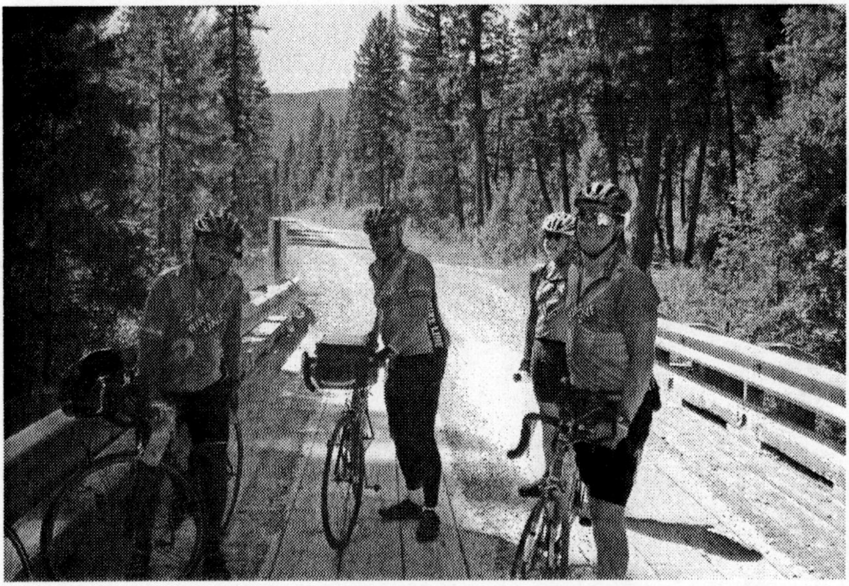

Day 7

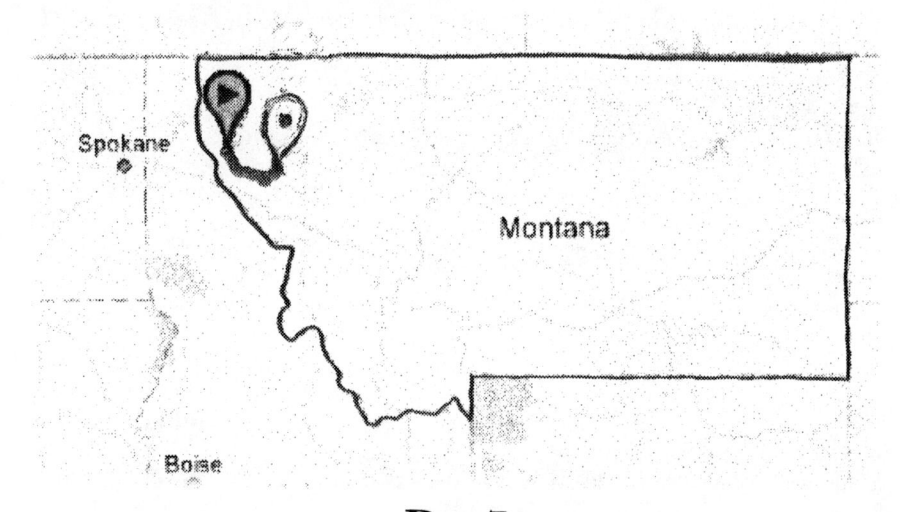

8/20 - Montana

"I wouldn't want to be me right now."

We left Trout Creek after breakfast en route to Whitefish and rode through both the Lolo National Forest and the Flathead National Forest. Mark worked with Ray on mapping our course, and we took a shortcut that we knew would be a dirt road. We didn't know it would be a 40-mile dirt road. Let's just say that riding a road bike on a dirt road is a bit different from riding on a paved road. Amazingly, none of us got a flat tire!

When we ran out of water, we went down to some of the mountain creeks and filled our water bottles. During a long stretch with no creeks, Ray asked a park ranger for some water, and she was kind enough to give us some. During the ride, I became so delirious that I said, "Oh, I wouldn't want to be me right now." J.P. and I cracked jokes which helped pull ourselves through the ordeal. As we traveled on the dirt road, we invented some skits for *Saturday Night Live* that I still think would really be good. At any rate, we laughed a lot. Given the added challenge of the dirt road, we needed those laughs.

After about four hours, we hit paved road again and ate at a restaurant near McGregor Lake. We met some great people there, and one couple wanted us to stay at their home for the night. This wasn't the first or the last time that perfect strangers would offer us a place to stay. Unfortunately, they lived in the opposite direction; and we stayed instead at the Hillside Hitching Post in Marian, Mont. We had ridden 98 miles.

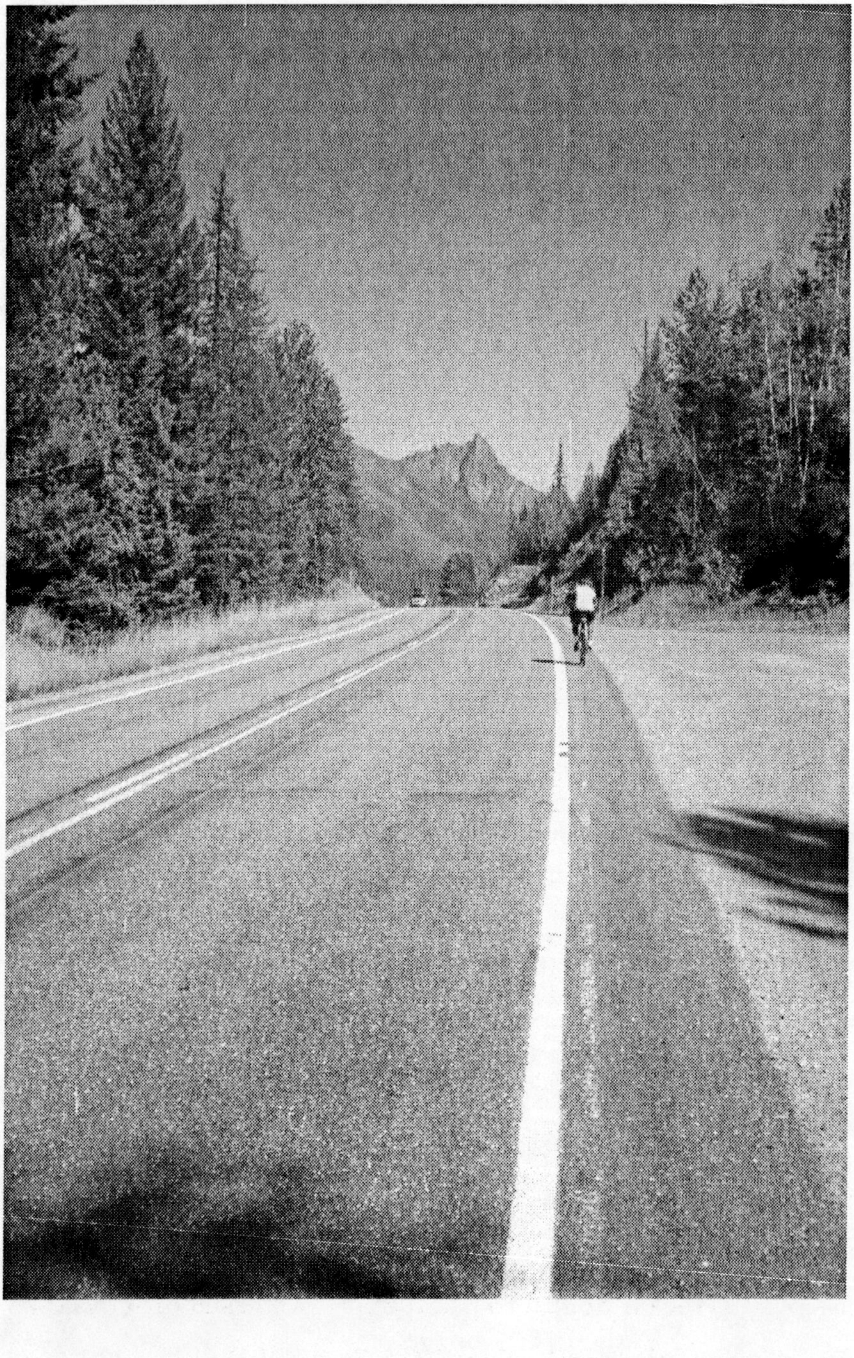

Day 8

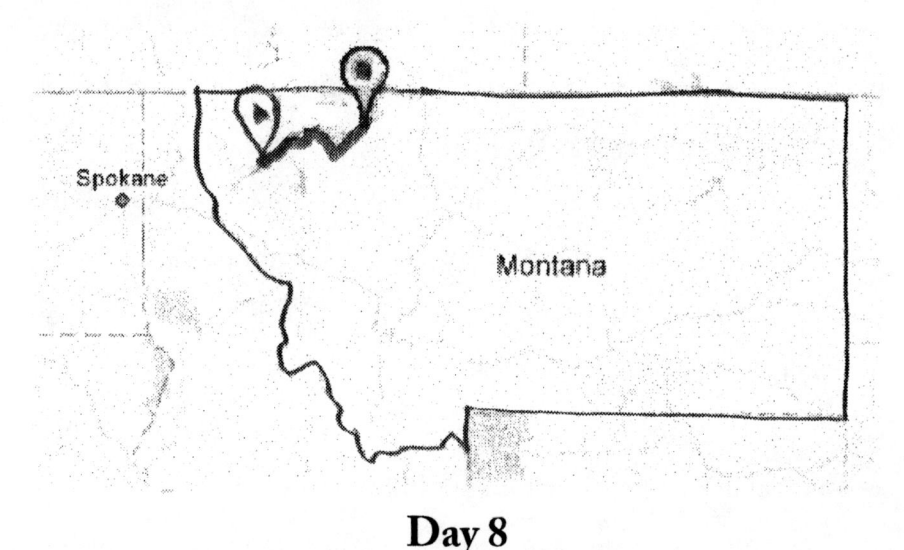

8/21 - Montana

Crossing the Continental Divide

The next morning we set out for Glacier National Park and had breakfast in Kalispell, Mont. From our hotel you could see the Rocky Mountains far off in the distance. After breakfast, I rode over train tracks without getting my bike properly aligned, and I went down on the pavement. Bike shorts do help to minimize injury when you go down; and, though I bled, it wasn't a big issue. Luckily, my bike was okay. I still had almost 3,000 miles to ride.

We crossed through a small town called Hungry Horse. The sign as you entered town had a picture of a horse on it that reminded me of the cartoon character Quick Draw McGraw.

J.P. was the only one who had the energy and stamina to ride up the "Going to the Sun Highway" in Glacier National Park. People say it is one of the most beautiful places on earth. Based on the postcards and pictures I've seen of different spots in the park, I know why Montana is known as the treasure state. The rest of us took the most commonly traveled route through the park and ended up in East Glacier. West Glacier, the town by the park entrance on the west side of the Rockies, was very nice; but East Glacier was drastically different. It was part of the Blackfoot Indian Reservation, and you could not drink the water. I suspected it was because it was such a small town in a remote location, but I never asked.

One thing for sure: We had some fantastic pizza for dinner that night, along with bottled water. On this trip you never knew if the food was exceptionally good or if we were just exceptionally hungry.

It was ironic that we could not drink the water because we had just crossed the Continental Divide. I had heard of the divide before the trip, but I didn't understand its significance. In the Americas, the Continental Divide separates the flow of water between the Pacific and Atlantic oceans. Precipitation that falls on the east side of the Divide flows toward the Atlantic Ocean; that on the west, toward the Pacific Ocean. We had ridden 109 miles. It snowed in Glacier National Park two days after we passed through.

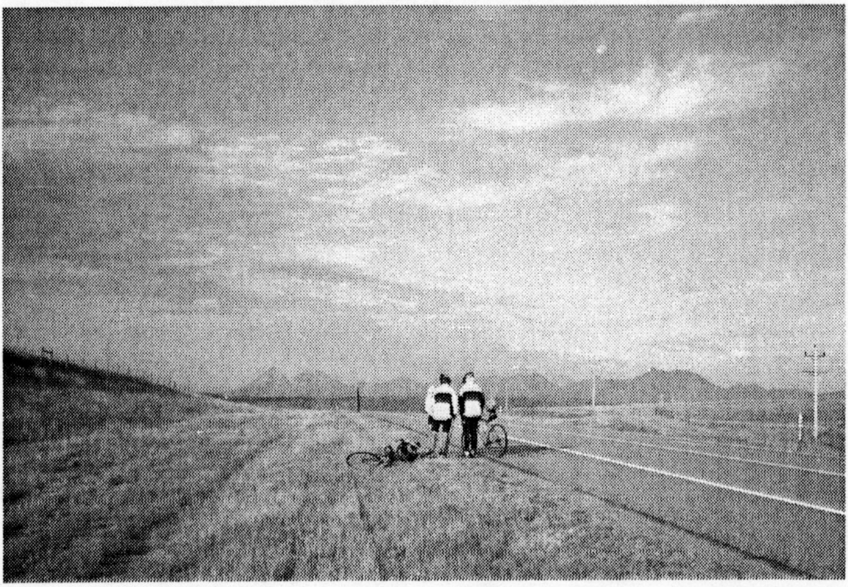

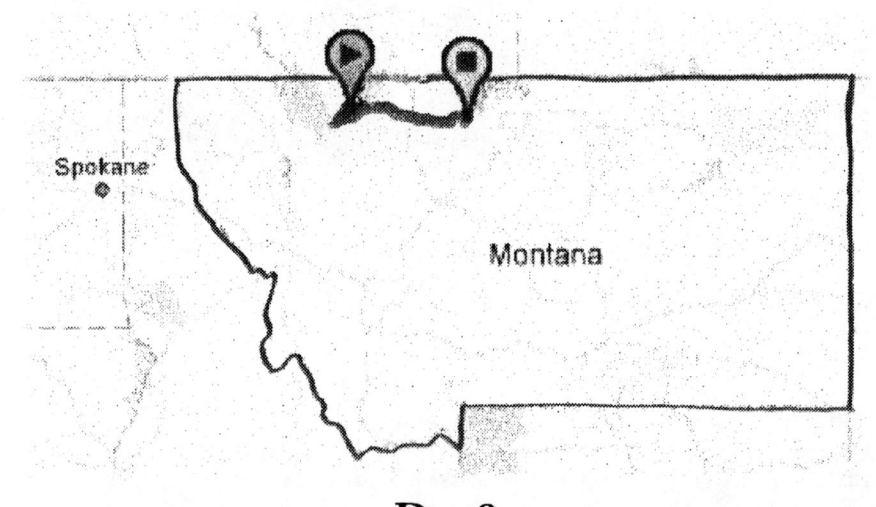

Day 9

8/22 - Montana

"My body hurts so bad I'd like to trade it in."

With our goal being Chester, Montana, the next day we set out for Browning for breakfast. Still on one of the Indian reservations, it was the dirtiest stretch of road I think we encountered on the whole trip. A dead horse on the side of the road looked as though it had been hit by a car. The town of Browning was depressing. When we stopped for breakfast, we locked the bikes up. This was the only time we locked up the bikes on the whole trip.

That day, for the first time, we had a strong tailwind; and we practically flew to Cut Bank, Mont., for lunch. Since we were making good time that day, I left the group with J.P. and went to the local library so he could download digital pictures for our Web designer, Joe Kihm, to post on our website, www.C4ride.com. I usually took an afternoon nap on the side of the road, but today I napped at the library. Luckily no one kicked me out.

I rode strong all day; but, in the last 42 miles, from Shelby to Chester, the wind shifted and the tailwind became a headwind. This is always a problem, especially in an area that is flat and open. Montana is known as the Big Sky state, and we were clearly on the east side of the crest of the Rockies. J.P. and I fell behind, and it was dark before we reached our destination. To make matters worse, we couldn't get a signal on J.P.'s cell phone. Towns in this part of the country are about 30 to 40 miles apart and usually consist of a grain elevator and not much more. There is nothing in between but farm fields.

Ray and Larry, who had arrived in Chester about an hour ahead of us, were worried. Ray was getting ready to send the sheriff out to look for us. J.P. and I got to Chester just as Ray was requesting the sheriff's assistance. Our bodies ached from head to toe. We also found out that day that there are rattlesnakes in this part of Montana. Needless to say, the daily afternoon naps on the side of the road stopped when we began to see large snakes that had been run over by cars. We had covered 115 miles of riding.

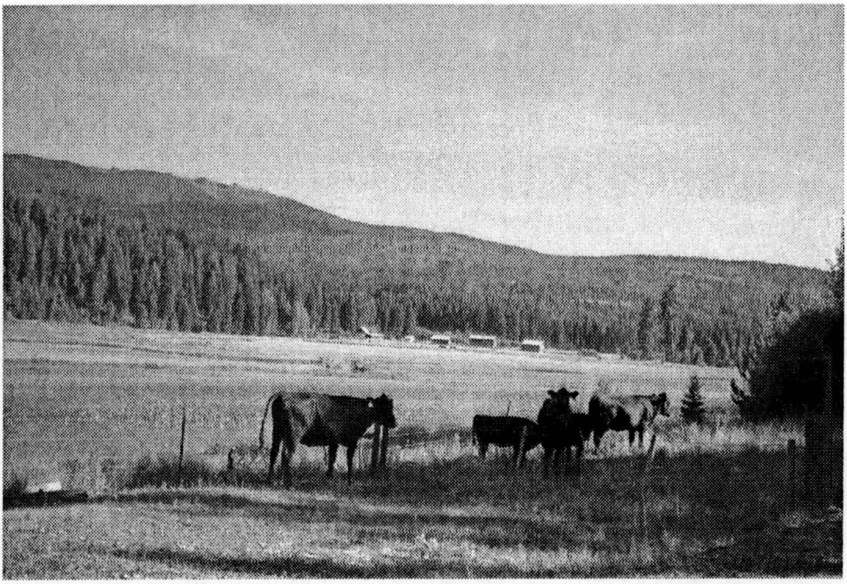

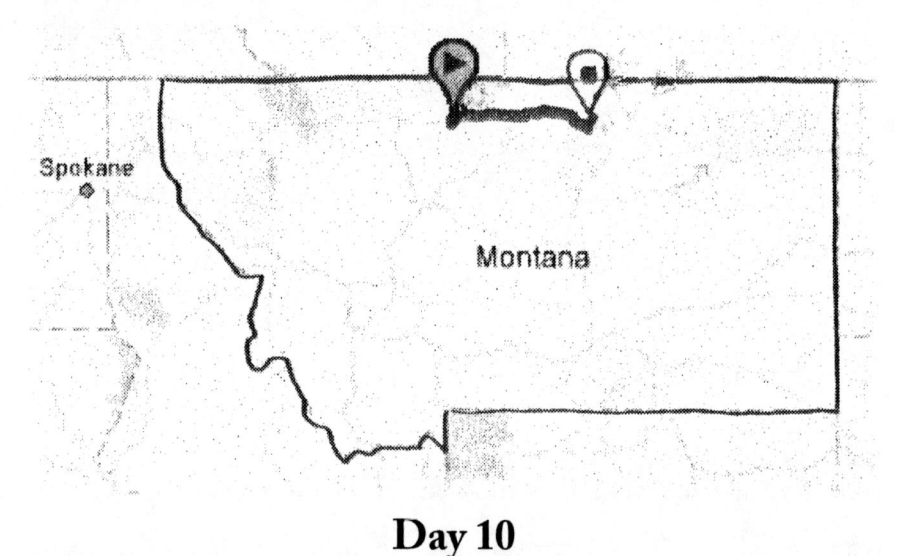

Day 10

8/23 - Montana

"It's beginning to take a toll on us."

We left Chester and rode to Harlem, Mont. Due to all the wear and tear over the previous days, the morning ride was hard for me physically; and I didn't want to be out there then. It was below 50 degrees each morning, making it even more challenging, especially the first half hour while we were warming up. I tried to keep myself warm as best I could. By afternoon, the pain had subsided for the most part, and I was into the ride.

We met some really nice people along the way. Montanans are incredibly down to earth, outgoing, and friendly; and they showed a genuine interest in our mission. We rode 100 miles for the day, and the weather in the afternoon was great; but, as we neared our motel for the night, we saw some black clouds racing our way. We no sooner got to the motel than a strong wind kicked up and the black clouds reached us. It proceeded to rain "cats and dogs".

At this point we were one full day behind schedule. Because we had so much riding ahead of us and the days had been more challenging than expected, I began to accept the fact that I might not be able to make the whole trip, since I had already accounted for all of my vacation days. A Greyhound bus was only a phone call away.

The terrain had been a combination of flat prairie and rolling hills. Ray had gotten his own room and awakened very early. He was ready to go at 4:30 a.m. This was just one more sign that the trip was beginning to take a toll on all of us.

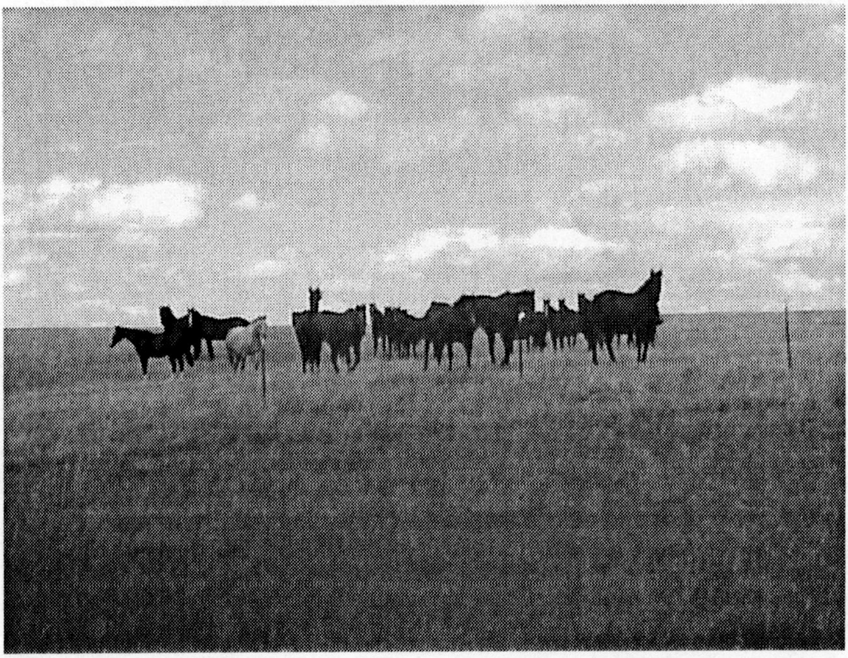

Day 11

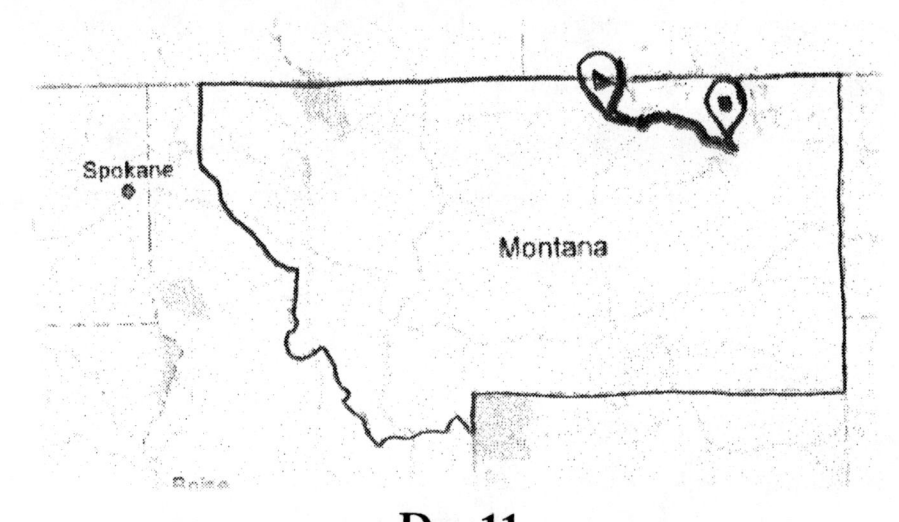

8/24 - Montana

Four flats in one day

We left Harlem and rode 114 miles to Glasgow, Mont. Early that morning I had a flat tire, and there was a minuscule piece of metal in the tire I couldn't detect. So three more flats followed. That night I had a tube-patching party.

The day's saving grace was a strong tailwind, and we absolutely flew. I felt like an Olympic athlete, and I began praying for a tailwind every day. I was also open to having the earth slant slightly to the east to make the whole ride home downhill. Unfortunately, we had none of that.

That evening, Elaine negotiated some coupons to have dinner at a local restaurant. Trivial things like this got us excited. Tomorrow we would leave Montana, after a long journey through the biggest state of the 14 we would cross, and enter North Dakota. I remember as a little kid being fascinated by Montana and always wanting to go there. Aside from not seeing a herd of wild horses running through the countryside, it was everything I hoped; and the people were even better!

Larry composed a haiku while riding:
Butterflies dancing
Floating gently with the wind
Slowly as lovers.

He was thinking of his wife, Mary Ann, whom we would see in North Dakota when she joined the team to take over the support vehicle. Larry is truly a romantic guy. Unfortunately, that trait provided no benefits for me.

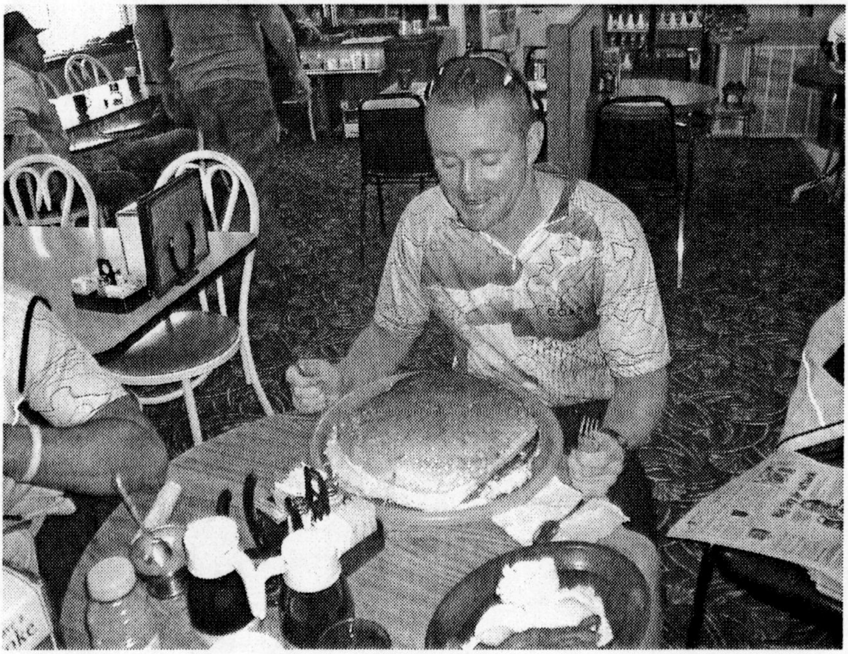

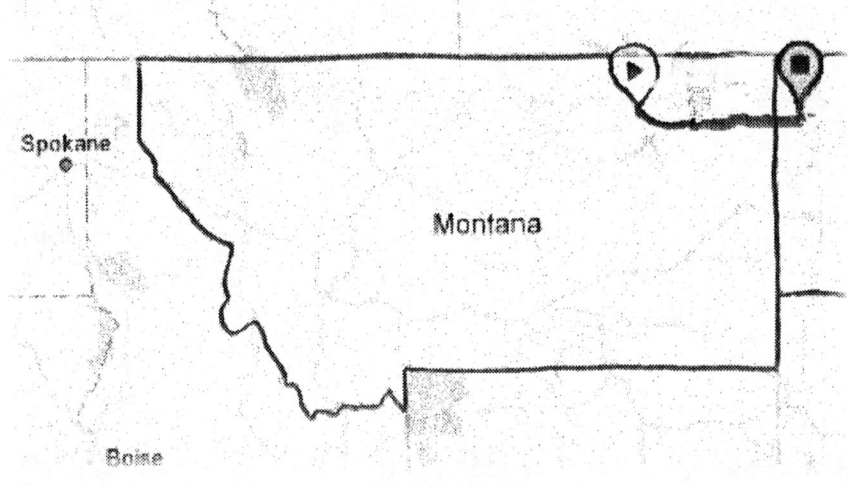

Day 12

8/25 - Montana and North Dakota

"Can I have chocolate chips on those pancakes?"

We rode from Glasgow, Mont., to Williston, N.D., today. Once again we had a strong tailwind, and we rode incredibly strong. We covered 147 miles for the day in only six-and-a-half hours of riding. I hit a max speed of 42.4 miles per hour, which was a personal record up to this point. If the wind had been against us, we would have been in big trouble. We were still aching, but we were feeling a little better than we had on day nine.

I had a flat tire again early that morning when one of my patch jobs failed. Tim and J.P. helped me change it. There were too many chefs in the kitchen. When we got the tube on and inflated, we discovered the tube was twisted. This is an example of six hands not being better than two. We didn't notice the problem until the tube exploded with a sound like a gun going off.

This was another example of the absolute need to find humor in every situation. If you were unsuccessful in finding humor at a time like this, it would mean big emotional trouble for you and those around you. I did find it humorous, but I'm not sure Tim did. He is very safety conscious.

We met up with Larry and Ray at Bergie's in Nashua for breakfast, and it was here that J.P. ordered the Biker's Trek Breakfast. He had two huge (pizza-size) chocolate chip pancakes, three eggs, and bacon. J.P. asked for chocolate chips every morning on his pancakes. I began to imitate him. Bergie's made homemade ice cream, so I had some ice cream for dessert after my breakfast and told the owner how much I enjoyed it. The owner and his daughter proceeded to bring me servings of four different flavors of ice cream. I didn't complain; I love ice cream. Ray, who had established himself as my ice cream-eating friend, had already left; so he missed it.

Another emotional lift for the day was that the time zone changed to Central Standard Time. We had now covered two time zones and three states over the course of the trip. It made me feel like we were really making progress, even though we had just entered North Dakota, which is a considerable distance from home! The Super 8 Hotel where we stayed that night had an indoor pool, hot tub, and a free drink from the bar. We thought we had died and gone to heaven. That was one of the best-tasting Coronas I've ever had. It was a good day!

We were still a day behind schedule, and I remember saying, "This trip is the most physically and emotionally demanding thing I have ever done." To this day, I stand by this comment.

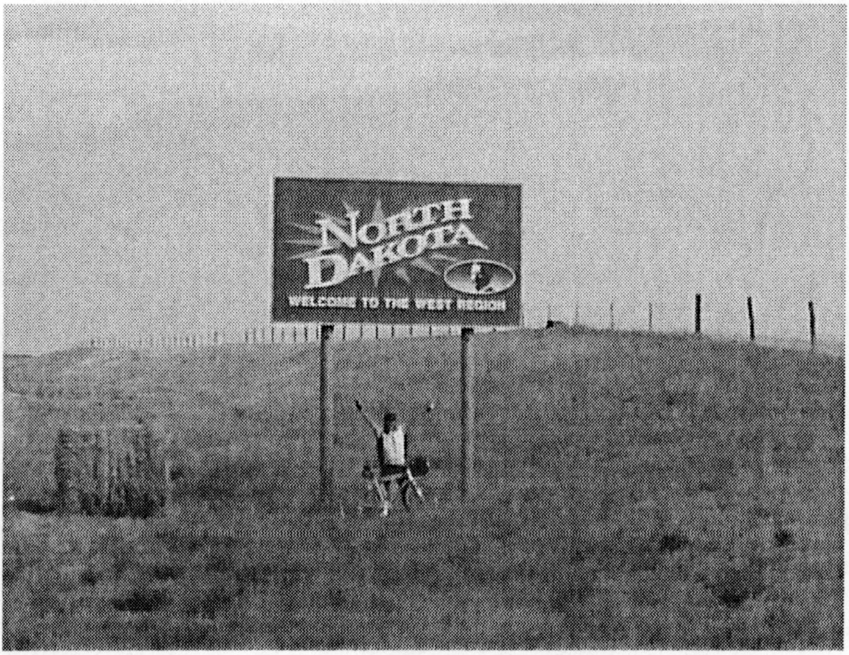
NORTH DAKOTA
WELCOME TO THE WEST REGION

Day 13

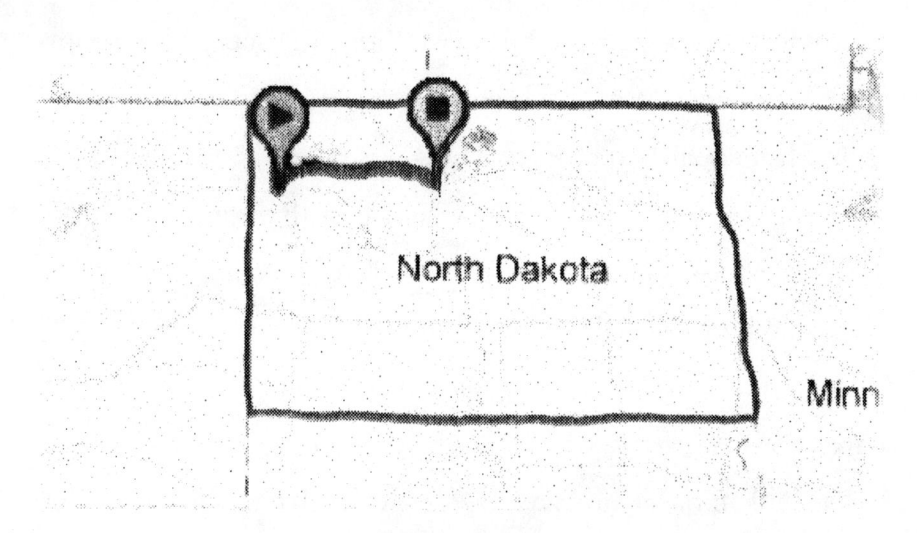

8/26 - North Dakota

Racing an antelope

Today we rode from Williston, N.D., to Minot, N.D. We covered 137 miles and had a tailwind again— thank God! The terrain was a combination of open range and plains, and the main crops were wheat and sunflowers. It was strange for a guy from the East Coast to see farm fields of sunflowers that went on for miles. Instead of riding with us, Tim and Elaine went to the Badlands. The rest of us didn't go because it was a longer route with more hills. While Tim was riding, an antelope came out onto the road. The antelope turned in the same direction Tim was riding along a fenced-in area, and they raced for about a half a mile. That story later made the newspaper back home.

A big event happened at breakfast. Larry, the poet and romantic of the group, announced that he had developed Indian names for each of us. His presentation of these names was hilarious. He named me *Wooshiki*, which translates as "man who rides with the wind." Because of all my flat tires, it later came to be translated as "man who rides on flat tires." Larry named J.P. *Totankapoo*, which translates to "buffalo breath." He named Ray *Golopagump*, "one who eats a lot." We named Larry *Chief Rotsaruck*, which translates to "one who needs lots of luck to pull off riding his bike across the entire United States." Quite honestly, we all needed *rotsaluck*. Since Tim was in the Badlands, he didn't get a name.

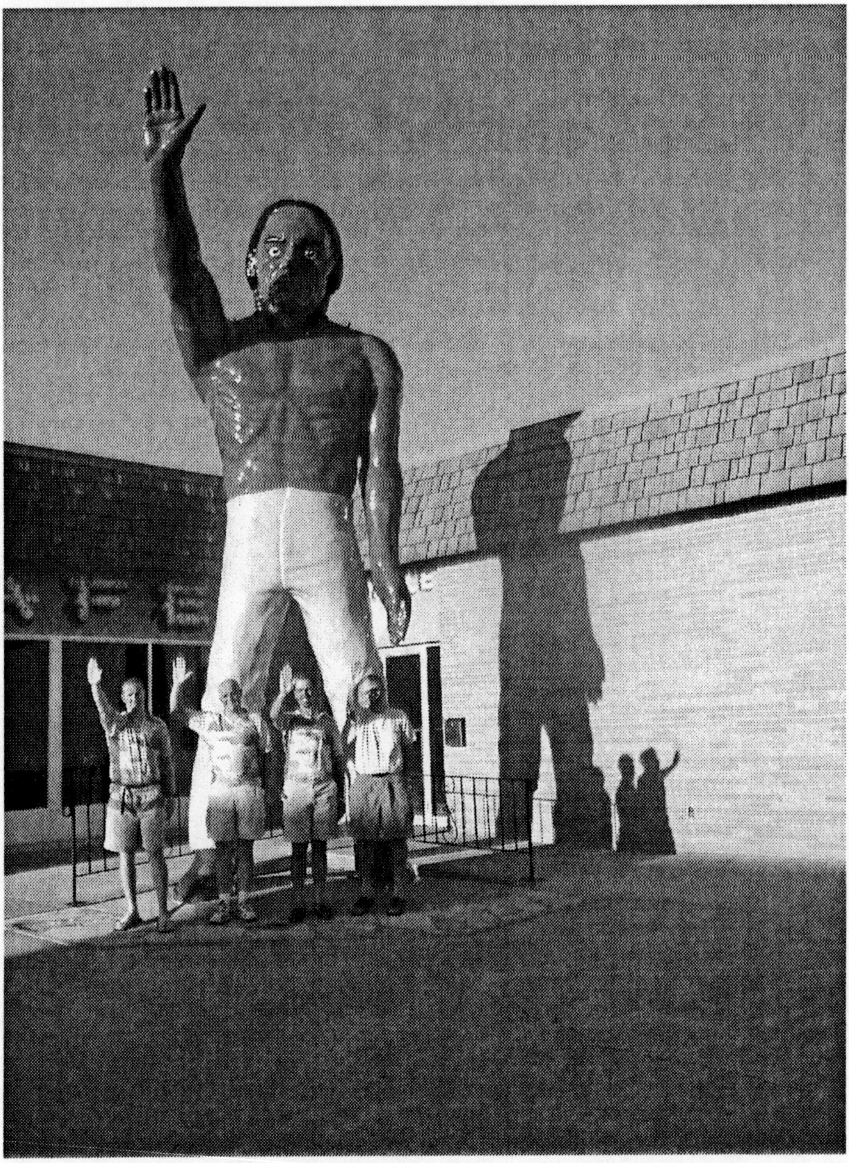

Day 14

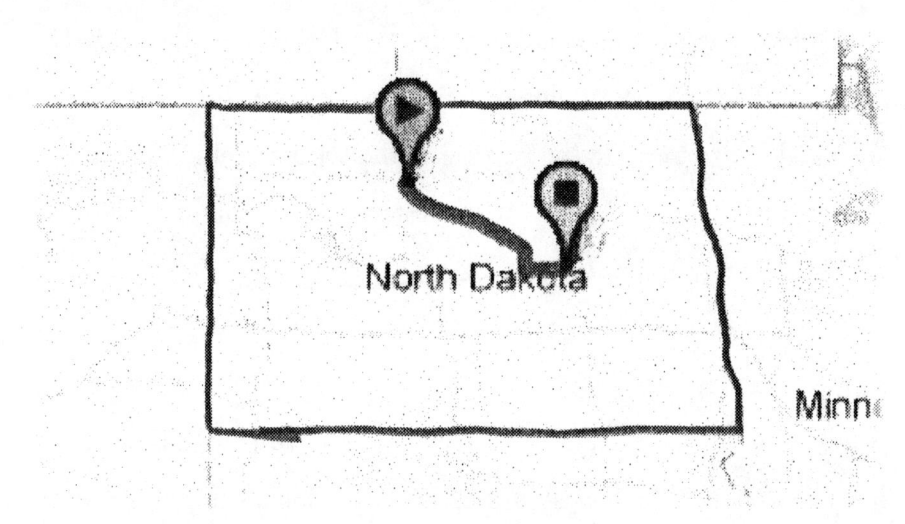

8/27 - North Dakota

The passing of the baton

Today we rode from Minot to Carrington, covering 130 miles. North Dakota is known as the Peace Garden State. I looked this up on the internet when I got home from the trip. On one of the crossing points between the U.S. and Canada, there is a garden to signify the peace between the two countries. The wind cooperated with us during the day's ride, but not as it had the previous day. We had ridden 528 miles in the last four days.

This was a big day because we were to meet Mary Ann, Larry's wife, and her friend Pat in Carrington. Larry was excited, to say the least. They were emotional when they saw each other, and it was great to see them united. I really missed my family.

Unfortunately, Elaine had to go back to Delaware. She had been key to the trip up to this point, and she posed for a picture with Mary Ann and Pat to indicate the passing of the support vehicle baton.

There was a huge Native American statue in front of the restaurant where we had dinner. This was a good photo opportunity.

We also received the bad news that J.P.'s uncle had died of lung cancer that day. After speaking with several family members, J.P. decided he would complete the trip; and the funeral was delayed until his return. We dedicated the next day's ride to J.P.'s uncle, Ray Albertson.

J.P. and I laughed a lot during this trip. J.P. says I'm a comedic genius when I'm stressed. Based on my stress level, I must have been hilarious. He dubbed me his "brother from another mother."

Ray and I kept eating ice cream together, and by now some pretty heavy trash talk had started about an ice cream-eating contest when we got home. I said I would do my talking when it came time to eat ice cream. I came to realize just how competitive Ray is.

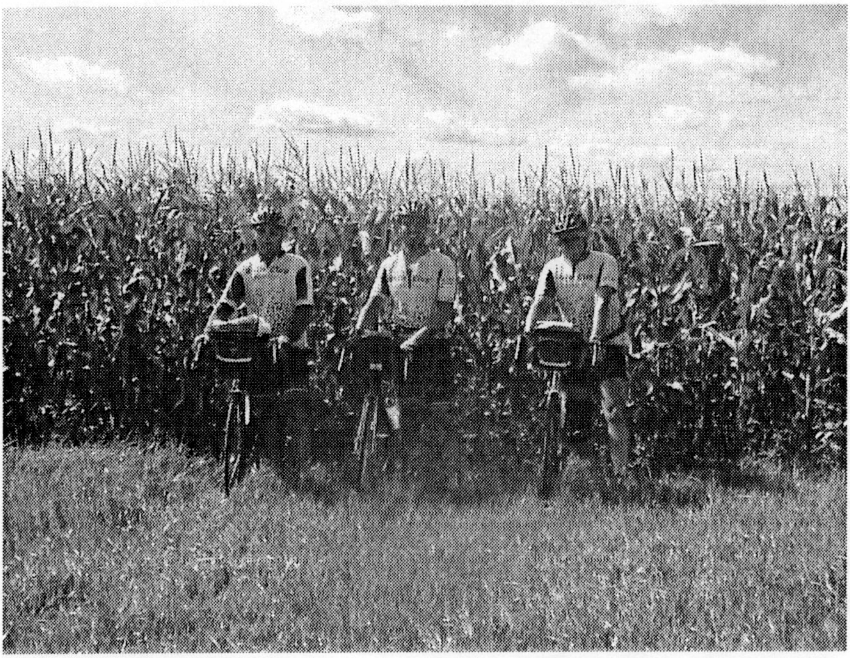

Day 15

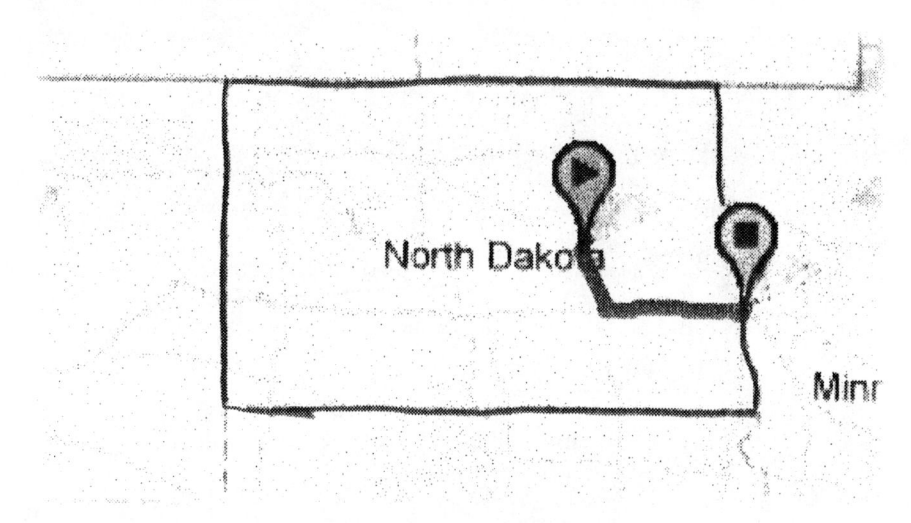

8/28 - North Dakota

The midpoint of the trip

The next day's destination marked the mileage midpoint of the trip. We left Carrington and reached Fargo, N.D. While it was a significant milestone, I couldn't believe we had another two weeks ahead of us. We rode 145 miles on this day, and I was beat. We had covered 559 miles in the last four days and 673 miles in the last five days. We had a side wind for a good part of the ride. That was challenging for me, especially after those days when the wind had been at our backs.

Up until now, the two constants we saw every day of riding were the Santa Fe Burlington Northern railroad and the drive-through espresso stands in almost every town we went through.

Over dinner that evening, J.P. told us that there was a poster of us at the Helen F. Graham Cancer Center. That was a surprise to me, and the news made me feel as though our efforts were getting some recognition. Little did I know how huge the poster was and that it was being used by the cancer center to track our daily progress across the country. I was touched when I found this out at the reception following the ride, where Dr. Nick Petrelli, the director of the cancer center, said that tracking us daily inspired the center's cancer patients.

(J.P., Larry, Amber, Ray, Rob, and Tim)

Day 16

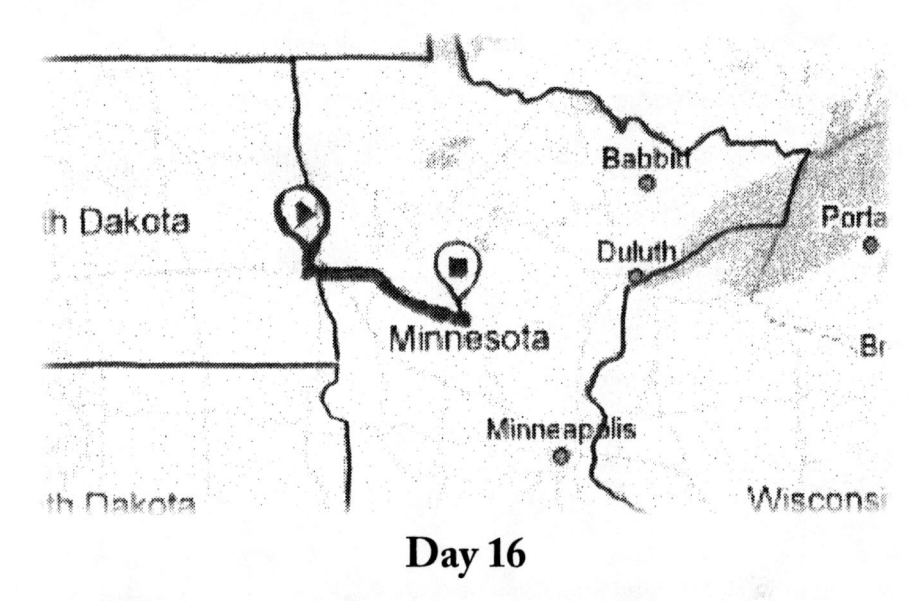

8/29 - North Dakota and Minnesota

"Yeah, sure, you betcha"

We rode from Fargo, N.D., to Staples, Minn., entering Minnesota, the land of 10,000 lakes, shortly after the day's ride began. It felt good to enter another new state, and we had a late breakfast/early lunch in a little town named Hawley. As it had been every day during the trip except one, the weather was glorious.

Our waitress at breakfast, Amber, was great. J.P. had a habit of asking the local people for sayings that were unique to each state where we were, and Amber told us that Minnesotans were known to say, "Yeah, sure, you betcha." When times got tough, I just kept saying that line out loud in my best Minnesota accent. Once again, the stress was showing.

We saw a lot of blond, blue-eyed people in Minnesota, which has a large Norwegian heritage. That day we were interviewed by a newspaper reporter in Hawley and one in Staples, and I began to feel as though I needed an agent. Not really! It did feel good that our mission and our efforts were getting some press that would help us to achieve our goals of awareness and fundraising. I certainly did not have a need for personal recognition, but it felt good.

That day I had my seventh flat tire. We covered 116 miles of riding.

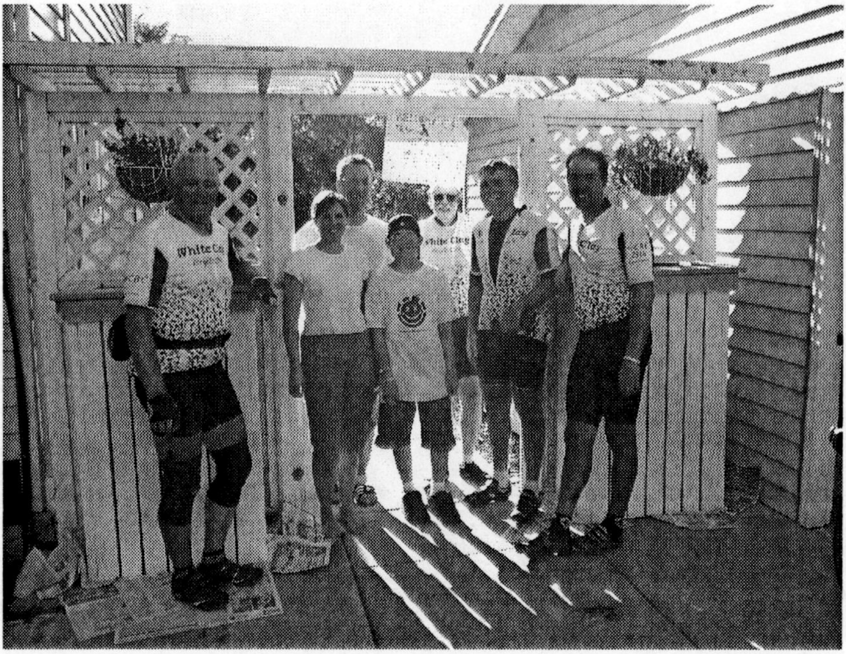
White Clay

Day 17

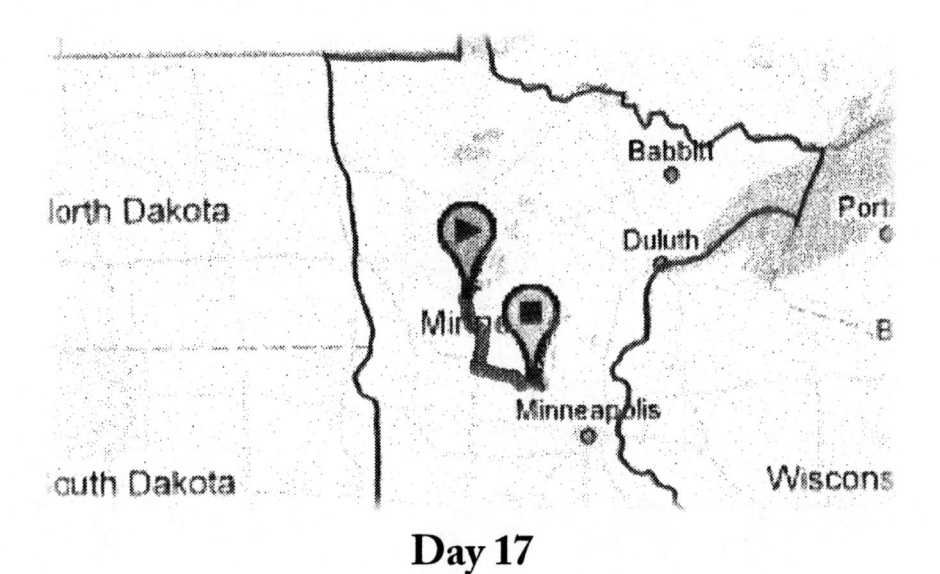

8/30 - Minnesota

Making us feel right at home

We rode from Staples to Clear Lake, and we had a directions screw-up. We were near a county line, and each county had a Route 8. We ended up on the wrong route and had to ride 101 miles instead of 85. We stayed with Paul Shlagel and his family. None of us had ever met them; but Paul was a contact through one of Ray's friends, and he invited us to stay with him in Clear Lake.

Paul and his wife, Julie, prepared a ton of food for us. Being cyclists and triathlon participants themselves, they knew just what we needed to eat to get refueled. I couldn't believe how much Paul ate. He has a slight but fit build, and he could out-eat any of us. Of course, he had not just completed a 17-day journey covering more than 1,600 miles.

He and Julie and their son, Kyler, could not have been kinder. They gave us their beds for the night and made us feel right at home. I had a flat tire the next morning, and Paul changed it for me. That was my ninth flat but only my first east of the Mississippi which we had crossed for the first time that day. I didn't know that that would be my last true flat of the trip. Mary Ann and Pat spent the night at a Benedictine convent in St. Joseph, Minn.

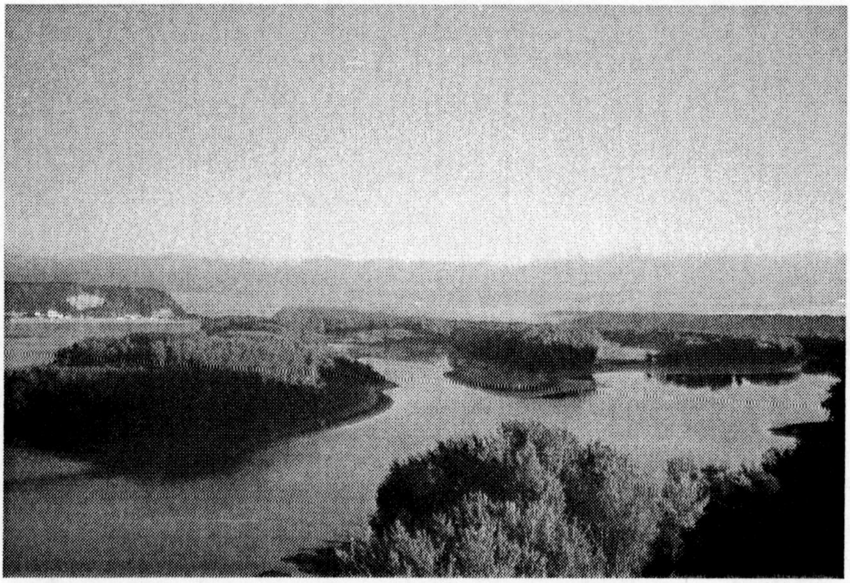

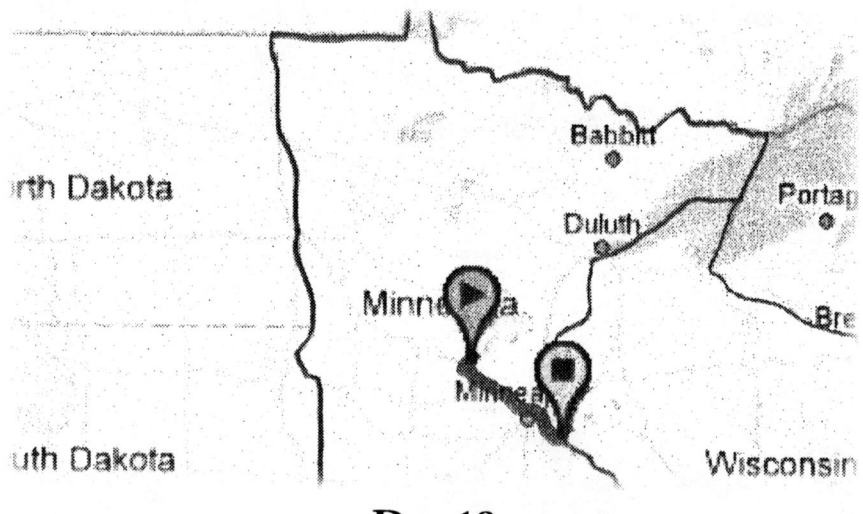

Day 18

8/31 - Minnesota and Wisconsin
The St. Croix River

We left Clear Lake, Minn., and headed for Prescott, Wisc. Wisconsin is nicknamed the Badger State. Late in the afternoon, we experienced only the second and final rain of the trip.

We were on some pretty big highways around Minneapolis/St. Paul, and we had to change our route a bit for safety reasons. We later crossed the St. Croix River. There were some beautiful developments along that river and some charming small towns. Most of the development appeared to be condos, townhouses, and other waterfront construction.

We covered 100 miles that day, and the Achilles tendon on my left foot was killing me. We still had nearly two weeks of riding ahead, and I worried about how bad the tendon might get. Luckily, the hotel we stayed in that evening had a hot tub, which helped the pain a lot. Vitamin I (ibuprofen) helped too.

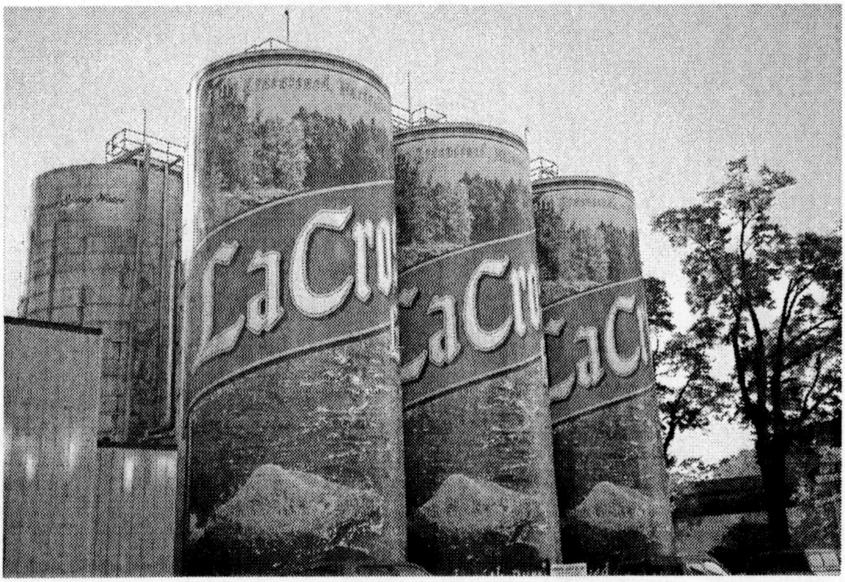

Day 19

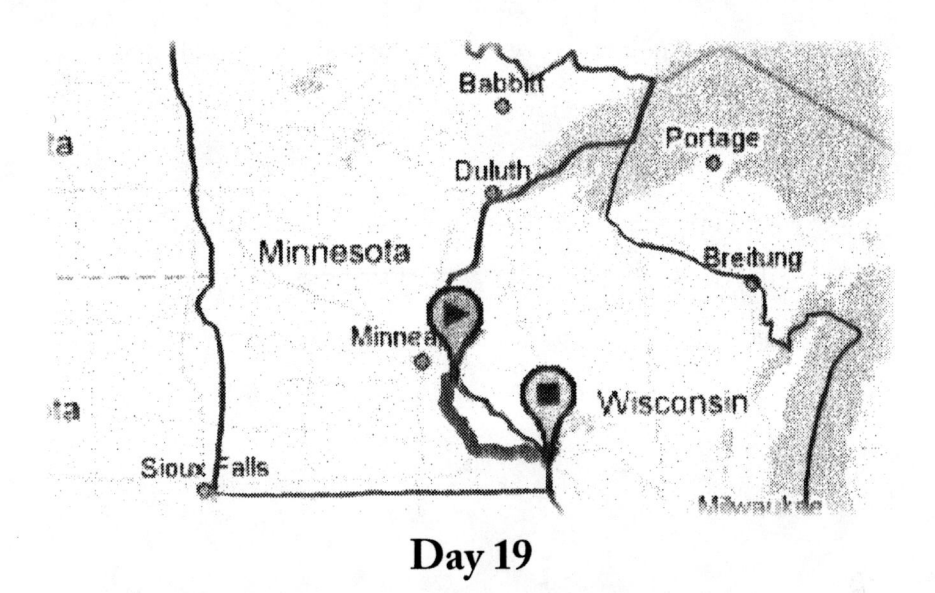

9/1 - Wisconsin and Minnesota

Bowling, anyone?

We rode from Prescott, Wisc. and ended the day in LaCrosse, Wisc. We had breakfast just over the Mississippi River in Red Wing, Minn. Red Wing is the town where the shoes are made by the company of the same name. We saw on the news that the Red Wing Shoe Company had produced a giant sneaker. It made the news because it had been transported to the Minnesota State Fair that week, so we unfortunately couldn't see it in person.

We rode on the Minnesota side of the Mississippi River for 115 miles, and I must tell you that the glaciers did a great job landscaping this part of the country. We rode through Lake City, which claims to be the birthplace of water-skiing, and through the Pepin Valley. The Mississippi River is very scenic in Minnesota, with bluffs on both sides and islands lined with evergreens dotting the river. It does not look anything like the river I always imagined Huck Finn rafting down.

We ended up spending the night in LaCrosse. We ate dinner at a bowling alley across from the hotel, and I seized the opportunity to bowl a game. Since all I had done for the last 19 days was bike, eat, do laundry and sleep, it felt good to do something different.

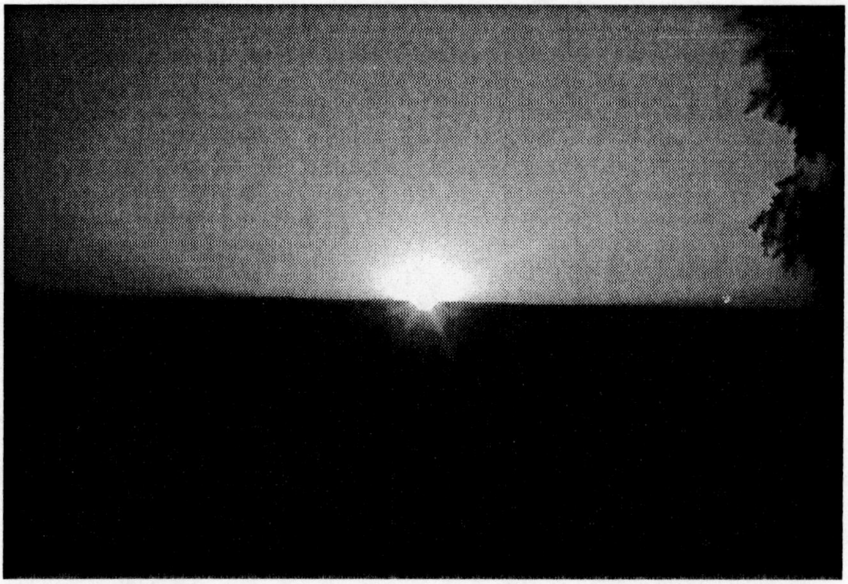

Day 20

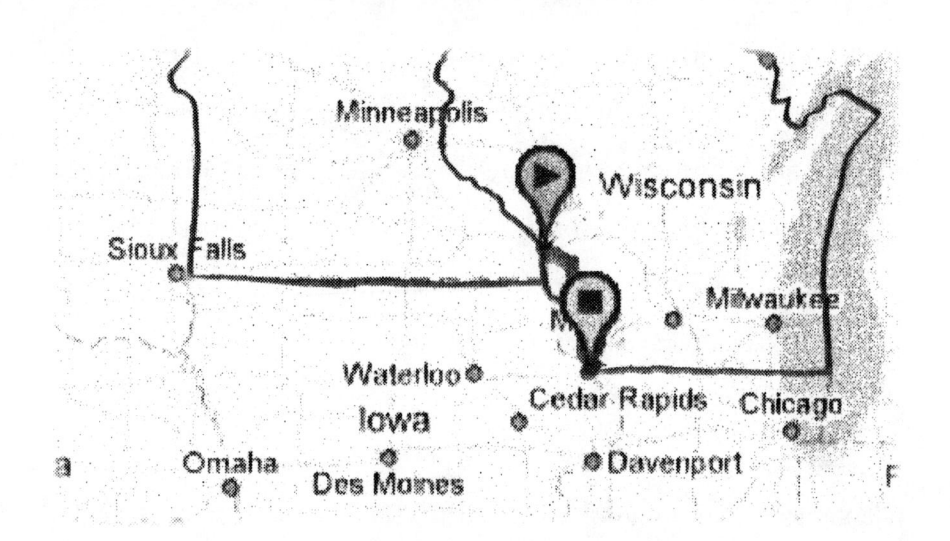

9/2 - Wisconsin

Character

We rode 107 miles from LaCrosse to Dickeyville. We rode along the Mississippi for the first half of the day, and it was great. During the other half we rode through Wisconsin dairy farm country. It was very scenic, but there were some challenging hills along the route. Toward the end of the day, Mary Ann stopped at the home of Jack and Helen, an elderly couple she met along the way. When the team arrived, Jack and Helen welcomed us all with homemade cookies and pitchers of ice water. As we left, Helen thanked us for stopping by and gave us the rest of the cookies. They were just another of the unusually kind people we met during the journey.

I roomed with J.P. that evening, and during one of the many conversations we had about the ride and how challenging it was, he told me the definition of character he learned in the Marine Corps: "The ability to follow through with something long after the joy, excitement, and novelty wear off." The definition had a lot of relevance to our trip and what we were experiencing. Quite honestly, I can think of a lot of important things in life to which it also applies.

Although I had sent my mother postcards, I spoke to her on the telephone that evening for the first time on the trip. She was glad to hear from me and told me she had been tracking me on the C4ride.com Website. While we were talking, she told me I looked rough; and she expressed her concern. I quickly responded that I appeared rough because I was. These had been the most physically demanding 20 days of my life. The fact that I was growing a goatee, and that it had a lot of gray in it, contributed to that rough appearance. We got a good laugh out of it.

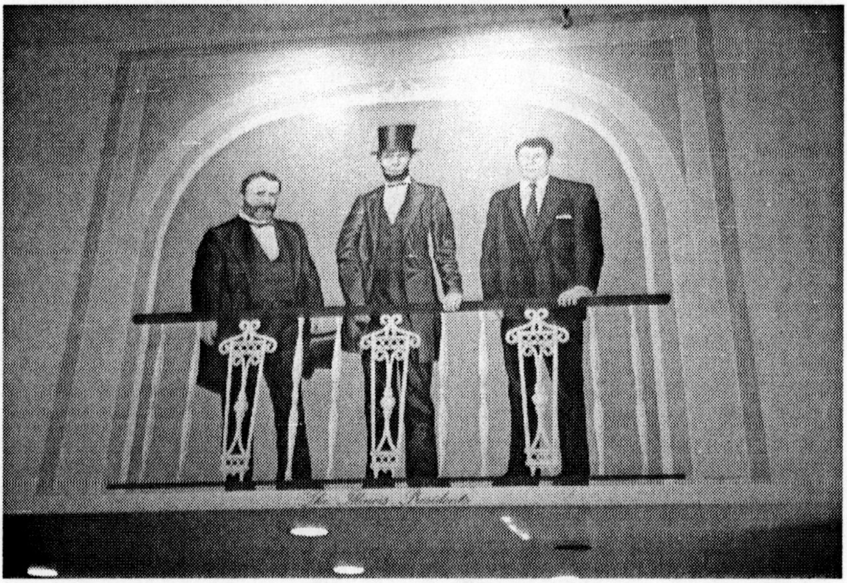

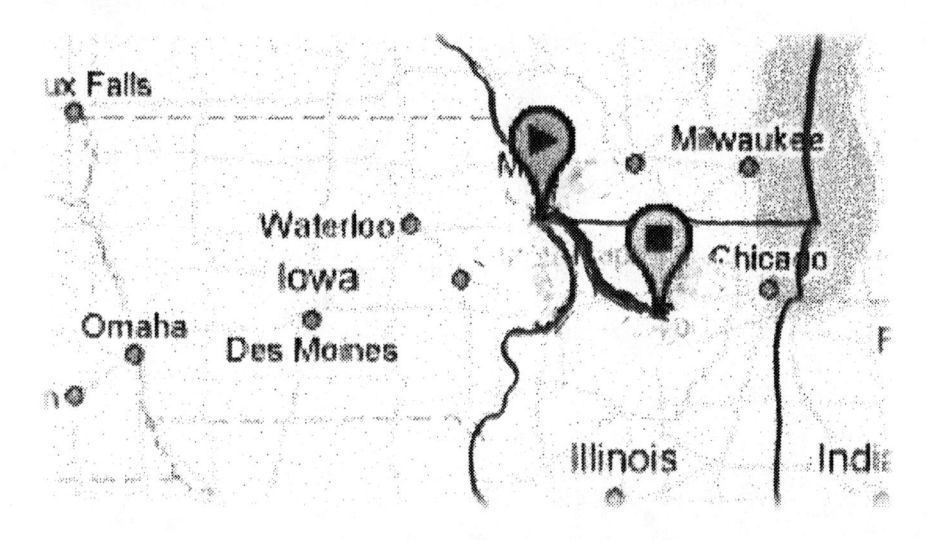

Day 21

9/3 - Wisconsin and Illinois
Presidential Pride

We rode 108 miles from Dickeyville, Wisc., to Dixon, Ill. We had entered the Land of Lincoln. Earlier in the day, we rode through Galena, Ill., the hometown of Ulysses S. Grant.

That evening we stayed in Dixon, which is Ronald Reagan's hometown. References to Reagan were everywhere. On the wall of our hotel was a mural of the three U.S. presidents from Illinois: Lincoln, Grant and Reagan.

Because the hills were so challenging for the first half of the day and we were running out of daylight, we fell 30 miles short of our objective of Mendota, Ill. So far, the scenic Illinois countryside looked just like Wisconsin. The sun was unusually bright all day, which made riding and the risk of dehydration a challenge. I remember thinking that it felt like summer for the first time during the ride— sweltering hot like late summer can be back home. We were not in the north anymore.

Our hotel that night had an indoor pool and computers with Internet access, which enabled J.P. to download pictures from his digital camera to send to our Web designer.

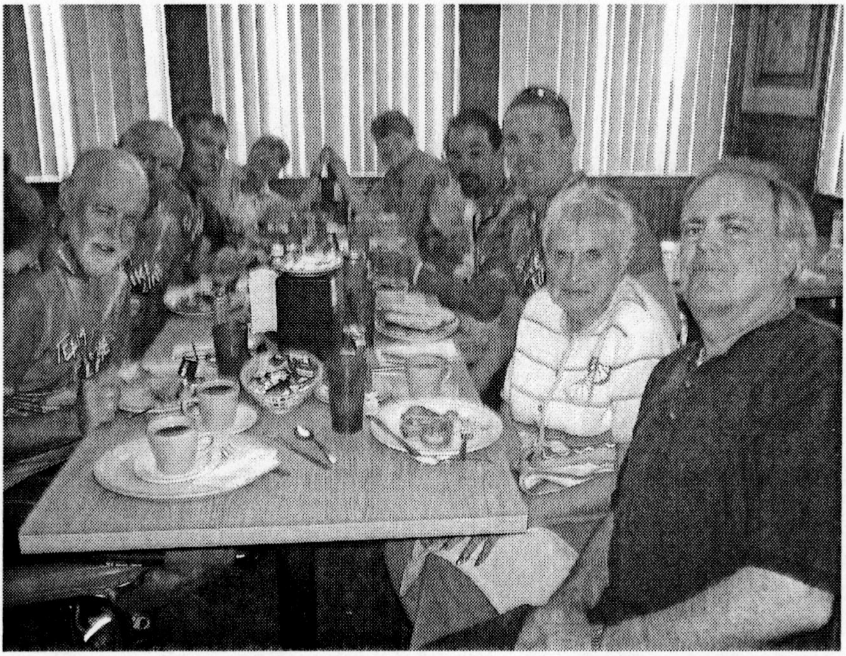

Day 22

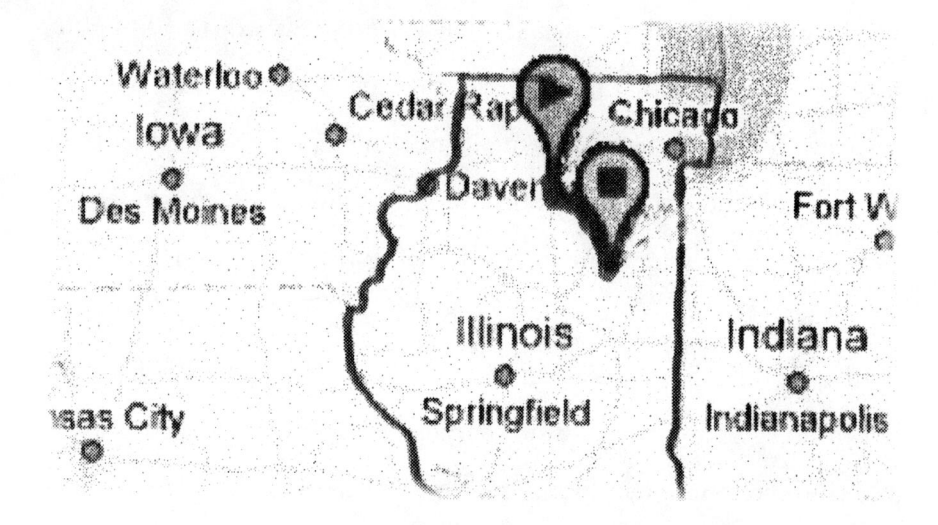

9/4 - Illinois

Breakfast with the O'Neills

We rode 104 miles from Dixon and ended the day in Pontiac, 20 miles short of our goal. We hit some strong headwinds. To make matters worse, in the middle of the day, I was literally falling asleep on the bike. That was scary and obviously dangerous. We also rode through the small town where Wild Bill Hickok was born.

That morning we had breakfast with Tim O'Neill's family. His mother and several siblings and their families drove to Mendota to meet us.

Following breakfast, while we were riding, I assigned lines for everyone to sing "High Hopes." This was the song that Southwest Air flight attendant had sung to us which became our theme song. I laughed so hard during rehearsal that I nearly crashed. I had to pull over because the tears of laughter got on my sunglasses and blurred my view. Stress was clearly taking its toll on me, but the laughter was good. Larry and I embarked on a humorous discussion about artistic differences, resolving the issue by agreeing that I would be creative director and he would be in charge of choreography.

I gave Tim the biggest line, "High apple pie in the sky hopes," but he struggled with it. I did it because I knew I had to give Larry and Ray the same exact lines, "He's got … high hopes." The two of them compete with one another constantly, so it was important to give them the same lines.

Our hotel that evening was near a Wal-Mart, and I bought three gallons of Gatorade. To help regain my strength, J.P. encouraged me to consume one gallon before bed, one gallon in the morning and one gallon during the ride the next day. I did as he had suggested, and I did feel stronger the next day. I also feel as though I could do a commercial for Gatorade now.

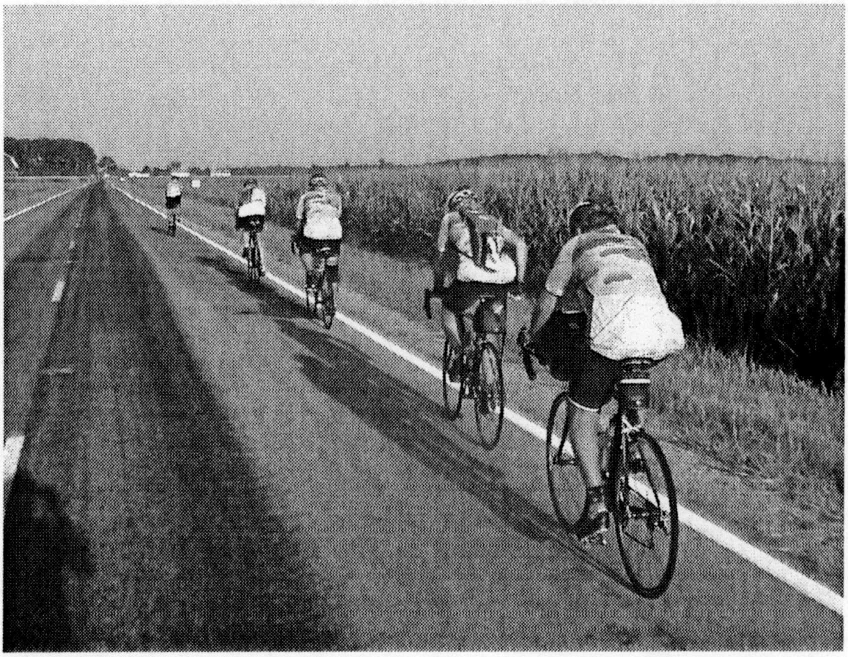

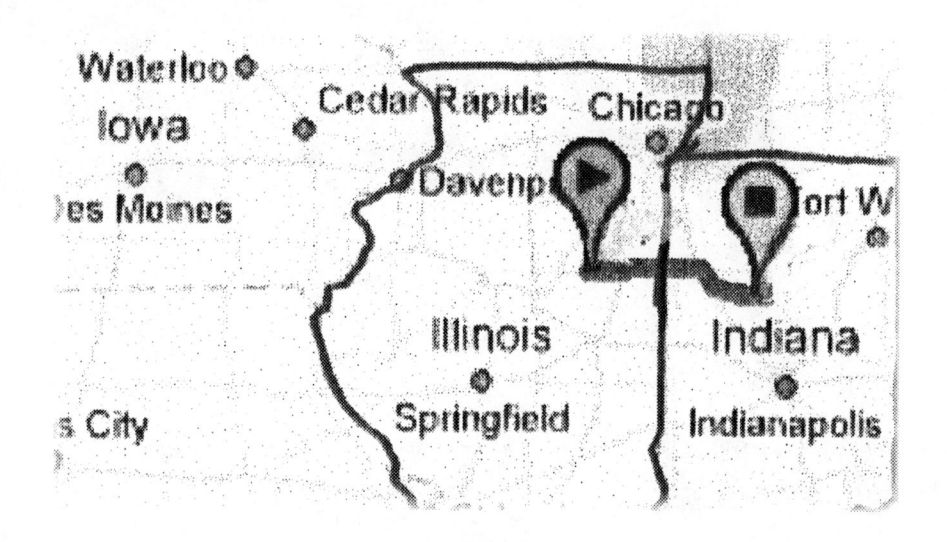

Day 23

9/5 - Illinois and Indiana

Get your kicks on Route 66.

Today was Labor Day, and we were one day behind schedule. We had a shot at making up a half day if the wind cooperated. It did, and we rode from Pontiac, Ill., to Logansport, Ind. We had made it to the Hoosier State. We had ridden for 12-1/2 hours and covered 142 miles for the day.

The 142 miles included a seven-mile screw up where Ray took me the wrong way down historic Route 66 until he realized his error. I think Ray had been taking too much vitamin I (ibuprofen) due to his knee pain, and it had begun to affect his brain. I should have realized the error sooner since the sun was to my right as we rode. We should have headed east, not north (you know, toward the Atlantic

Ocean; and the sun always rises in the east). I felt a little sorry for Ray because he said the worst part of it all was having to break the news to me about his mistake, based on my anticipated reaction. I was pretty easy on him.

On this day of riding, I had a problem concentrating; and I almost "wiped out" drafting behind one of the riders. Fortunately when I went off the road, there was high grass and a wide, flat shoulder for me to run into. I was lucky I didn't get hurt or hurt one of the other riders.

At dinner that night, a woman holding a baby opened the door for me. She was with her husband and another of their children. When we entered the lobby, the gentleman asked me why we were all wearing the same bike jersey. I explained as I had done many, many times before and gave him one of the slips of paper with the C4ride.com Website address. After his meal and while we were waiting for our dessert, he came over to the table. He was moved by what we were doing and had picked up our bill for dinner. Happily, I had just ordered dessert. We talked for about 10 minutes, and he explained that he was a family doctor with a local practice. It was great to talk to him and his wife. He told us stories about his medical practice and his success in identifying and treating cancer in his patients. He also took pride in telling us that Lance Armstrong had received cancer treatments in Indiana.

(Rob, Elton, Larry, J.P., Tim and Ray)

Day 24

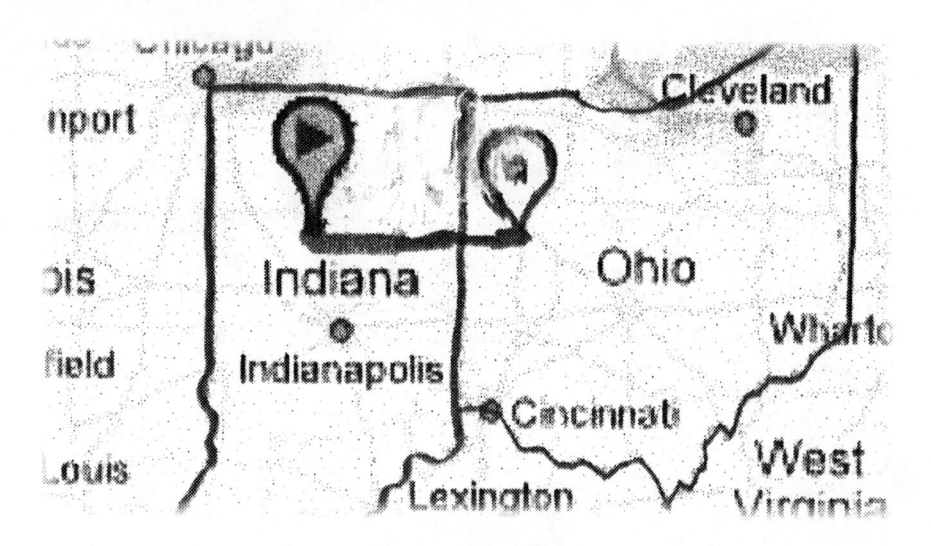

9/6 - Indiana and Ohio

Elton

Today we rode from Logansport, Ind., to Lima, Ohio. We covered 123 miles, changed to Eastern Standard Time, and entered the Buckeye State. It was really starting to feel like home. We spent the night with Elton Hammond, an 81-year-old gentleman who was a member of the local bike club who had heard about our efforts.

Elton was a retired engineer for Westinghouse and a graduate of MIT. He also served in the Army Corps of Engineers during his working days. Over dinner he told us about his father, who served as the chief signal officer for General Patton during World War II. He told us stories of his life growing up as a military brat. He cooked steak for our dinner and made a few phone calls to get a local television station to come out and interview us. We'd got some television coverage at home prior to the ride; but this was the first time we were on television during the ride, to our knowledge.

Elton rode with us for two days. We covered 175 miles, and Elton matched those miles with a $175 contribution to our cause. Elton was an impressive rider by anyone's standard, and especially for an 81-year-old.

(Jessica Bussom)

Day 25

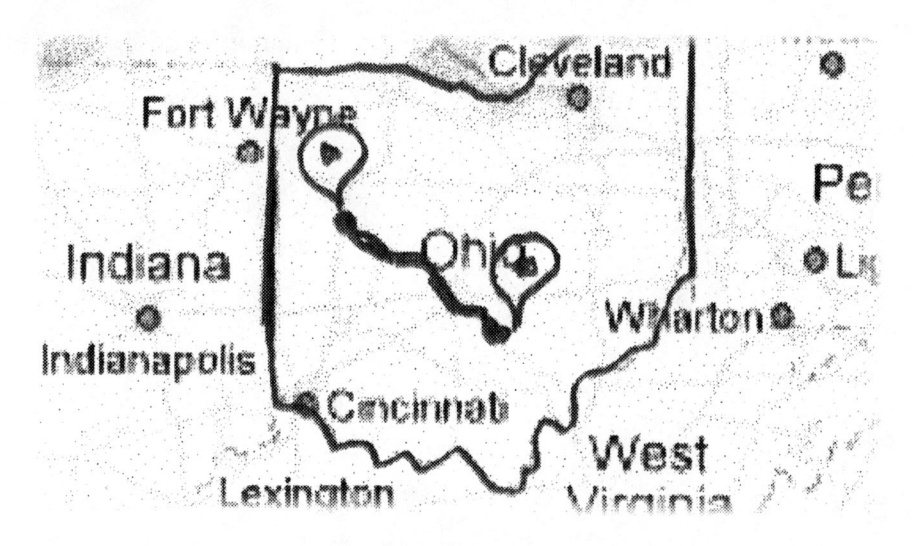

9/7 - Ohio

Back on schedule at last

We rode from Lima to Pickerington and covered 133 miles. We stayed with Ray's niece, Kim, her husband, Bob, and their four children on their small farm. Cynthia, Ray's wife, met us there and joined Mary Ann for the rest of the trip to assist with the support vehicle. The entire family was very friendly, and we really enjoyed our visit there. The dinner was outstanding, and we ate like farm animals ourselves.

Ironically; that day we rode close to Delaware, Ohio, and Newark, Ohio, which made me think of home. The greatest news of the day for me was that we were finally back on schedule. We had struggled for more than 20 days to make up for lost time, and we had finally accomplished it. Now we were only five days from home and six from the end of the ride. I remember thinking maybe there would be no need for a Greyhound bus after all.

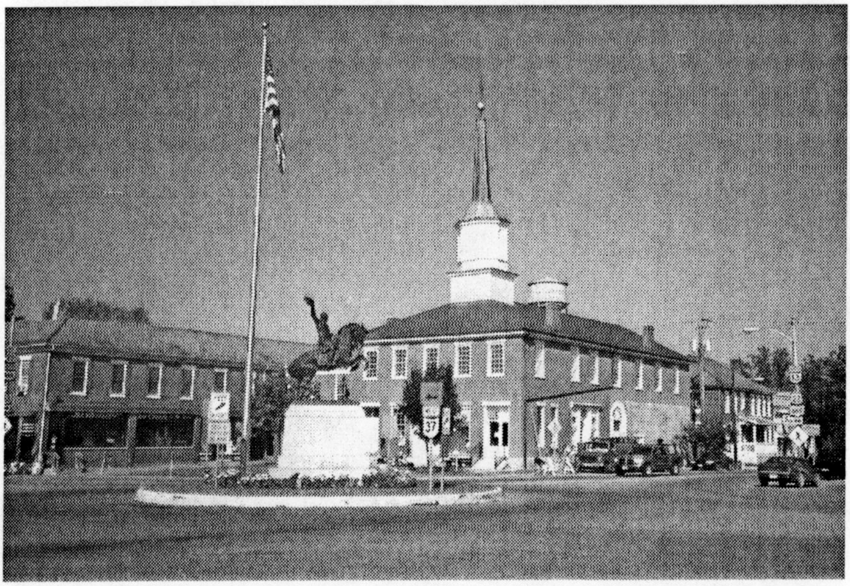

Day 26

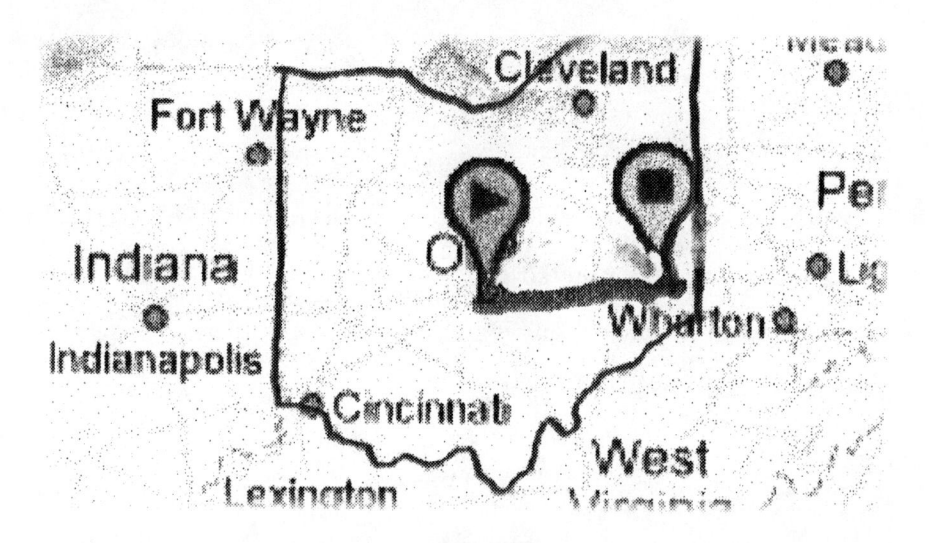

9/8 - Ohio

A Police Escort

After riding from Pickerington to St. Clairsville, Ohio, we were only 11 miles from the West Virginia state line. We covered 125 miles today. I didn't ride the last 20 miles because I broke a spoke on my back wheel. Since Ray's knees were hurting, we pulled over at a Dairy Queen and ate as much ice cream as possible until his wife, Cynthia, came to pick us up. Hanging out at a Dairy Queen after a long day of riding, knowing you can eat all you want and you'll never gain a pound, was like poetry in motion. The hills were brutal on this day of riding, and we were running late. Although these hills were not long, they were very steep.

Since it was dark, Tim, J.P. and Larry got a police escort for the last 10 miles of the ride, flashing lights and all. They loved that. This was also the day that Tim almost got run off the road by a mobile home that was being transported as an oversized load. Due to road construction, we encountered the same oversized load twice. That was a little scary. When I saw it coming the second time, I rode my bike off the road so I would not get hit.

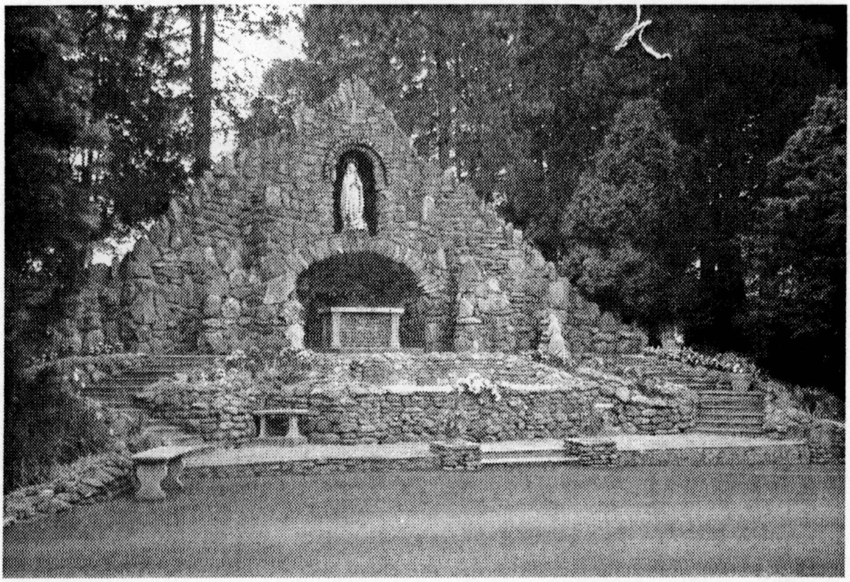

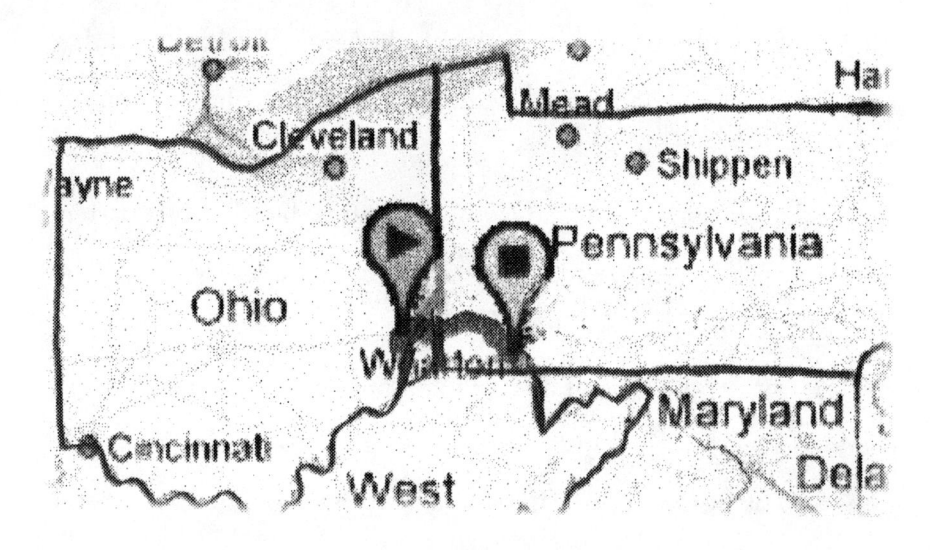

Day 27

9/9 - Ohio, West Virginia and Pennsylvania

A Night at the Convent

Today we rode from St. Clairsville, Ohio, through Wheeling, W.V., and on to Uniontown, Penn. We rode only 79 miles which seemed like a vacation. We had entered the Keystone State and actually stayed at a convent. Mary Ann saw the convent and asked if we could stay there for the night. Due to the cause for which we were riding, the nuns said yes. J.P. teased Mary Ann at dinner that night about knowing the secret handshake for nuns, since she had also stayed at a convent in Minnesota. I complimented Mary Ann on her consistently excellent negotiation skills and informed her that I felt she had the ability to strike a deal with the Pope. She indicated that her 12 years of Catholic school education may have played a role.

The monastery grounds were stunning. It was obviously an estate that had been sold or donated to the Catholic Church. The quarters were impeccably clean; and we left them clean, for fear we would be struck by lightening if we didn't.

We were at the base of a huge mountain range that was present everywhere you looked in the landscape of the town. At this point, we would be home in three days, and we began to let ourselves feel the excitement! I also began to allow myself to digest all the events since August 13, and it was overwhelming. Every day had been an adventure, but I was ready to get home.

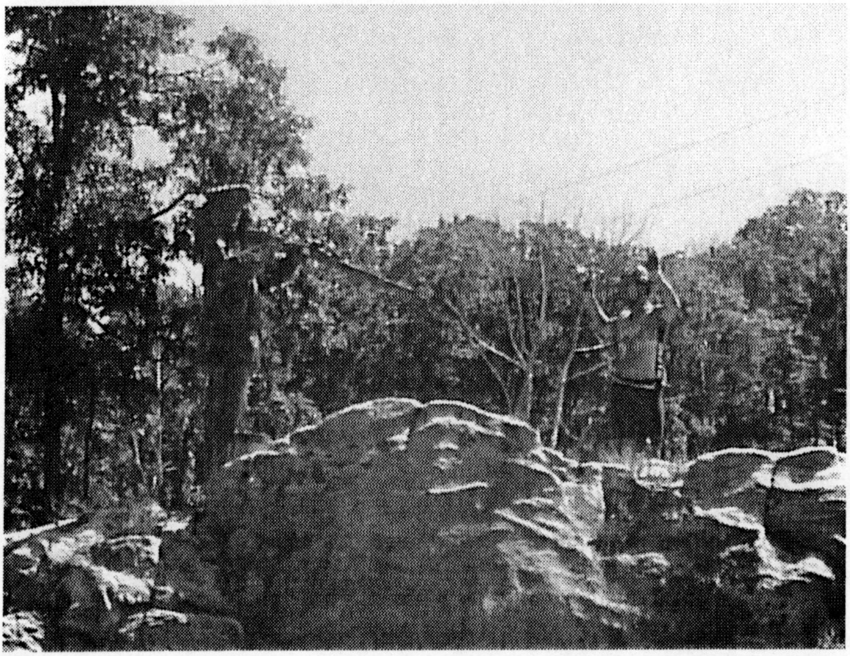

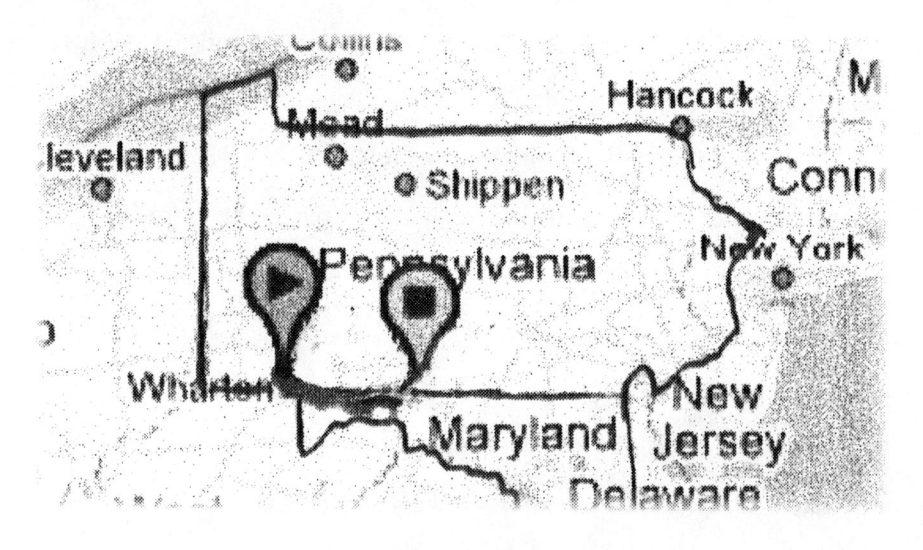

Day 28

9/10 - Pennsylvania and Maryland

Falling short of our goal late in the game

Today we rode from Uniontown, Penn., over the Allegheny Mountains and landed in Cumberland, Md. Maryland is nicknamed the Old Line State because it's heroic "troops of the line" won praise from George Washington during The Revolutionary War. It was great to see the state symbol that is so familiar to me. We rode only 67 miles for the day but covered the steepest mountains of the entire trip. We saw signs indicating as much as a 13 percent incline.

In the mid-afternoon, we reached Frostburg, Md.; and I stopped for some ice cream. Someone told me Cumberland was 12 miles away and all downhill. That sounded too good to be true, but it was. With the exception of one small stretch of road, it was 12 miles downhill. That felt great after a long day of riding through the mountains.

When we reached Cumberland, we discussed pressing on to Hancock, Md. It was 40 miles farther, but people in Cumberland told us there was no place to stay between Cumberland and Hancock. We figured that was probably inaccurate, but we decided it was too risky to press on in the few daylight hours we had left. Now we had to make up 40 miles in the last two days of the trip *and* cross the Appalachians which we understood were comprised of six mountains ahead. At any rate, the views for the day's ride were outstanding, as the western part of Maryland is very scenic.

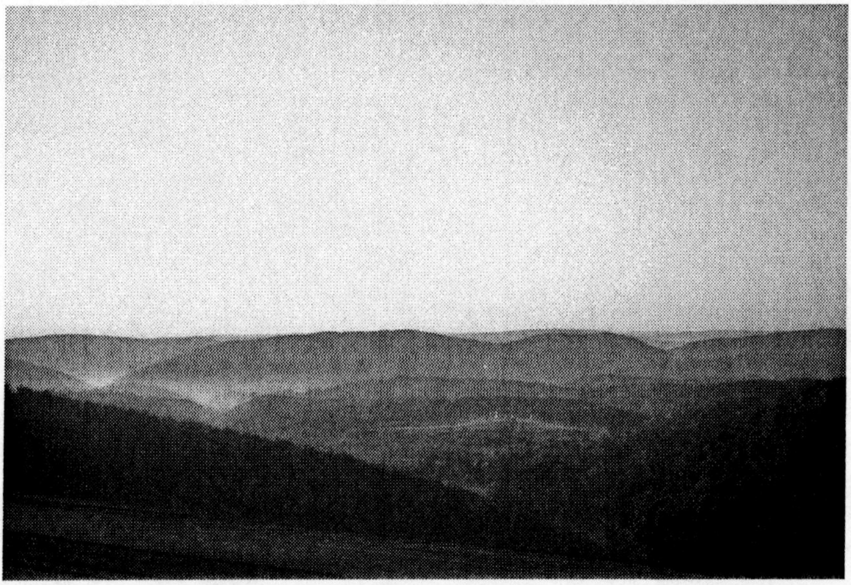

Day 29

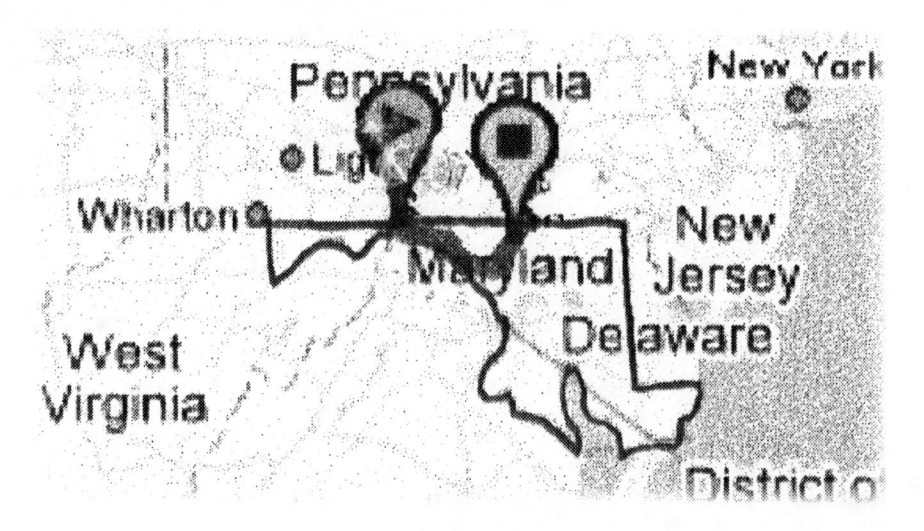

9/11 - Maryland

The last day of mountain climbing

Today we rode from Cumberland to Westminster, Md., and got back on schedule! We rode 110 miles and climbed all six mountains. It was a brutal day, one of the hardest days of riding for the entire trip. We started our ride at 6 a.m. in the dark, jumping on an interstate highway to avoid the highs and lows of the mountains ahead. We knew it was against the law to ride a bike on an interstate, but we did it anyway. Only seven miles up the highway, we got pulled over by a Maryland state trooper, who asked us to remove ourselves from the highway. We got off at the next exit.

Coming down the final mountain that day, which happens to be the one where the Appalachian Trail is, was fantastic, not just because I knew it was the last large mountain of the trip but because it was an especially fun ride. The road snaked for miles under an umbrella of trees; and I was moving faster than traffic, averaging about 30 miles per hour. It was an all-out sprint to the bottom, and I really laid into the corners. After more than 3,000 miles of riding that bike for 29 days straight, the bike and I were like one. It was an awesome, unforgettable ride down!

Tim and I stopped at the bottom, and I took a nap while we waited for the others. That night we met Alfreda and Bruce Clinton, friends from back home, at the hotel. It was great to see familiar faces, and they were kind enough to treat us to dinner. They were in awe of what we had accomplished and gave us updates on the reaction by the people at home regarding our ride.

Knowing I would see Terri, Anna, and Lauren the next day, after 31 days, was exciting! Also, the goatee was to come off tomorrow night, and my kids wanted to help me shave it off. I was ready to get rid of it.

(Terri, Anna, Rob, and Lauren Sorantino)

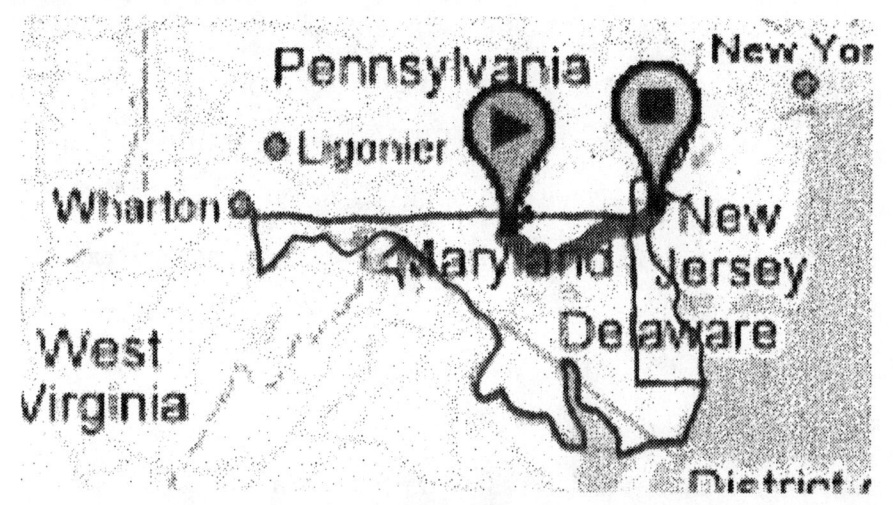

Day 30

9/12 - Maryland and Delaware

Home at last!

Today we left Westminster to go to Newark, Del.! The ride was an easy 80 miles to Delaware, the First State and home to each of us. Newark is also home to the University of Delaware, where I had graduated almost 20 years before. We rode directly to Bike Line on Main Street, one of our sponsors. Terri, Anna, Lauren, and Terri's father arrived shortly after we got there. It was a celebration, and people wanted to hear our stories from the road.

We then rode to Ray's place of business to make an appearance. The conclusion of the day was riding up Fawks Drive, and side-by-side, Ray, J.P., Larry and I rode across the finish line at J.P.'s parent's house. J.P.'s parents hosted a welcome home party for the team and their families, right down to the huge banner stretched across the street. We still had to go to Rehoboth tomorrow to touch our bikes in the ocean to complete the trip coast to coast, but we were home!

I stayed at the reception at J.P.'s for a while, then rode home. People thought I was crazy to ride my bike home when I could have gotten a ride. But that was a glory ride for me, one I had daydreamed about every day during the trip. Riding down Limestone Road, into our development, and down my street was every bit as good as I had imagined it would be!

Lauren, Anna, and I did shave my goatee off. Never having had facial hair before, I was surprised at how hard it was to get it off. It was great to see my family, but a little strange to be home, and I knew it would take some adjusting after the long, taxing journey and all we had experienced.

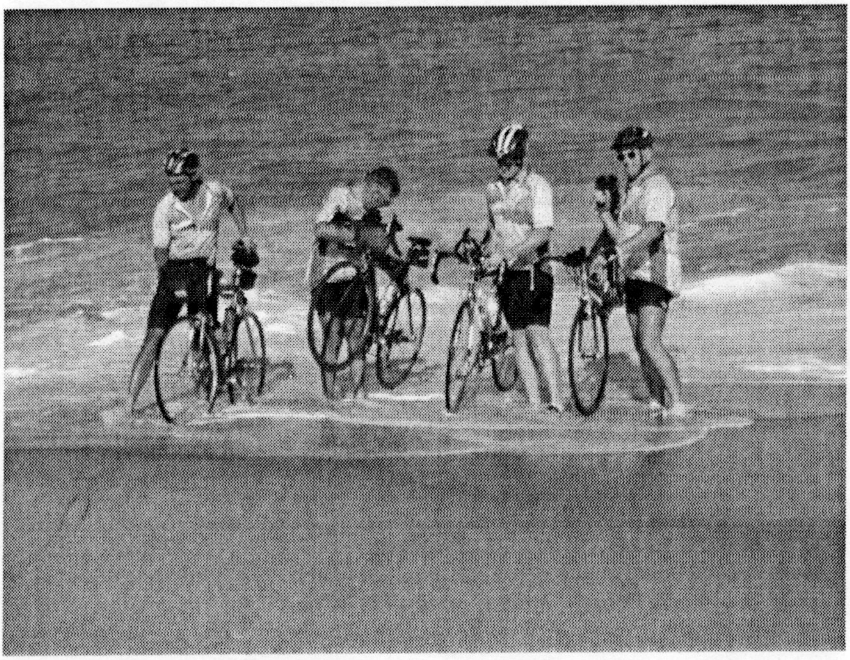

Day 31

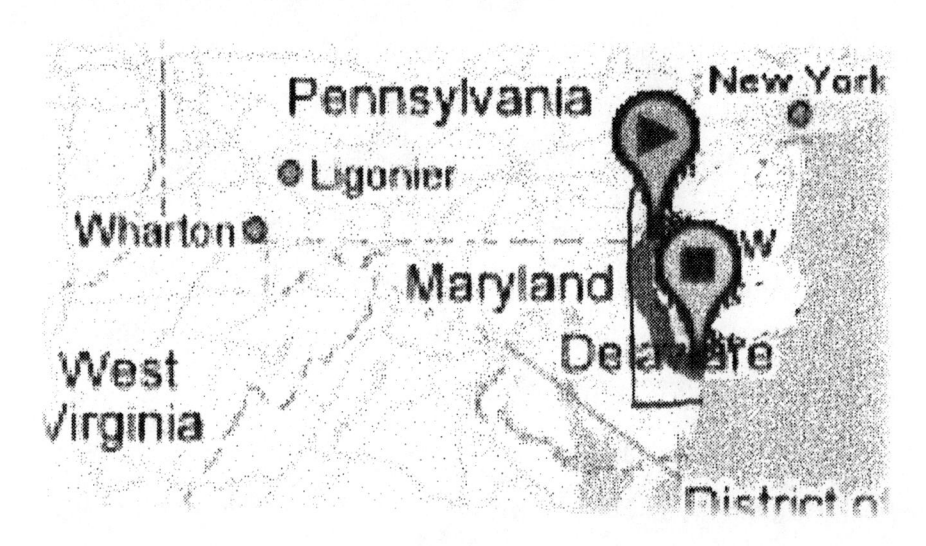

9/13 - Delaware

Reaching the Atlantic

I got up at 5 a.m. and went to Burton's Barber Shop to get a haircut. I'd felt like a hippie during the trip, with my straggly beard and longer-than-usual hair. I didn't even take a brush or comb on the trip. Since my hair is so thin, it was no big deal.

I arrived at Ray's by 7 a.m. and everyone commented on my change of appearance. All I needed were my glasses to complete my normal conservative look. We took off for Rehoboth Beach, Del. Unfortunately, the trip did not end without an accident. Only four miles from the Atlantic Ocean, one of the bikers who joined us for the ride that day swerved to avoid glass; and another biker ran into him. This caused a chain reaction; and four bodies flew through the air, including Tim and Larry. Tim and one of the other riders, Eddie, had to go to the hospital. Eddie has got to be one of the toughest 78-year-olds I've ever seen. He grew up in Brooklyn, N.Y., owned a construction company, and the women always make a fuss over him. Get the picture? Other than some stiffness he experienced for the next couple of weeks, Tim was fine. Eddie had to get some stitches, but both were released that night.

We later went back to the scene of the accident, a Grotto's Grand Slam Restaurant, and had all the pizza we could eat, "on the house". We ate nine pizzas. Several members of Grotto's staff, who had been very helpful immediately following the accident, invited us back for dinner that evening. The local news channel, waiting for us at the boardwalk, heard about the accident on the police scanner, came to the scene, and taped us there. But it wasn't the story it would have been. Now the story was about an accident rather than the accomplishment of riding coast to coast.

J.P., Ray, Larry, and I did make it to the boardwalk in Rehoboth as planned; and there was a crowd of people waiting for us where Rehoboth Avenue meets the Atlantic Ocean. We were a little late due to the accident, but there were still quite a few people waiting for us. We walked our bikes down to the ocean to dip them in the Atlantic. A color photo of the four of us dipping the bikes was on the front page of the *News Journal* the next day.

We had done it. We had ridden our bikes from the Pacific to the Atlantic in 31 days! It is something that very few people ever attempt, and we actually did it. Oh, how sweet it is! Reaching the Atlantic was a little different from what I expected. Rather than a loud celebration, we acknowledged the completion of the trip quietly and more individually than I expected.

As it had been for almost 31 days of riding, the weather was gorgeous and the ocean water was perfect. I put the bike down and took a swim. I swam out far and treaded water for a while. It was an amazingly satisfying feeling, but I remember thinking that what we had just done couldn't have happened. It didn't seem possible that I had ridden a bicycle from the Pacific to the Atlantic in 31 days. But deep down, I knew it was real; and I took the time during that swim to savor what we, and I, had accomplished. I knew I couldn't have done it without the encouragement and support of the other four riders and those who followed in the support vehicle.

Nonetheless, I couldn't help feeling I needed proof of what I had done to make it more of a reality than a dream. The pictures I saw over the next several days helped, but I realized at that point that using my daily journal entries to write a book would make it more real for me and for everyone who cared to take the journey with us by reading it.

Coast to Coast to Cure Cancer Bike Ride
MONTANA
Start
August 14, 2005
IOWA
5 cyclists ride to raise funds - and awareness - for the
Christiana Care Helen F. Graham Cancer Center

The Reception at Helen F. Graham Cancer Center

"The weather had to be divine intervention."

I went back to work the next day. J.P. was actually the only one of the original five to make the ride back to the Helen F. Graham Cancer Center from Rehoboth Beach. He was joined by several other local riders, some sponsors, and others from the center. I arrived at work that morning before anyone else did. Coworkers had decorated my door, and one of the pictures was Lance Armstrong crossing a finish line with my face over his. It said, "Welcome back Rob—congratulations! You are an inspiration to everyone who sets out to accomplish something that seems beyond reach. Your passion to find a cure has touched the lives of so many people. Your determination will forever be appreciated by the many people you helped."

Even as I write these kind words, I am touched by them. As Larry said several times during the trip, we set out to inspire people through our cause; but really we were the ones inspired by the many people we met along the way—especially those who had a direct or indirect experience with cancer.

I remember the day I graduated from college. It was the culmination of four years of hard work, and receiving that degree meant a lot. Having worked for a consistently successful company for many years and a company that was a good fit for me, I've also achieved some great things professionally—more than I ever expected at my age.

But I will tell you with certainty that I felt truly honored that day at the Helen F. Graham Cancer Center after our trip. Several days before the reception, J.P. said the people at the center had a plaque for us and asked me to invite a few family members for a "little reception." I wasn't expecting much.

I was able to leave work a little early that day, and I put on my bike gear so I could ride across the finish line with the group. Terri, Anna, Lauren and my mother, sister, older brother and his wife, mother, and father-in-law all came to the event. There were a lot of people there. We joked about feeling like celebrities or rock stars during the trip, but today we really did feel like we had done something important. After we crossed the finish line, we went inside the center.

As we came indoors, Queen's song "We Are the Champions" was playing, and everyone cheered for us. We went into a reception room where we got a lot of positive attention from people. There was a large poster of us at the front of the room, along with the map of the United States with the various stops along the way. It was modeled after the map Lauren, Anna, and I had designed before I left for the trip so they could track our progress. I had shared copies with each rider's family and Mike Chalmers from the *News Journal,* and it got used a lot in the public eye.

We were asked to take our seats at the head table while Dr. Petrelli made some comments. When I sat at the head table, I was glad no one spoke to me because I had a huge lump in my throat. I didn't need to look to see that the other riders did too. We were emotionally drained from the long, hard ride. We glanced at each other with sincere, proud, and humble looks and enjoyed the wonderful comments being made.

Addressing the audience, Dr. Petrelli said that although there had been previous events like this one at the cancer center, this was the most important. He talked about our mission and its impact on finding a cure. Each of us received a plaque that symbolized our accomplishment, and then we participated in a question-and-answer session. It was ironic that after 32 amazingly nice days with about a total of four hours of rain during our more than 300 hours of riding time, it began to rain like "cats and dogs" during the reception. It was like a message from above that we had achieved our mission.

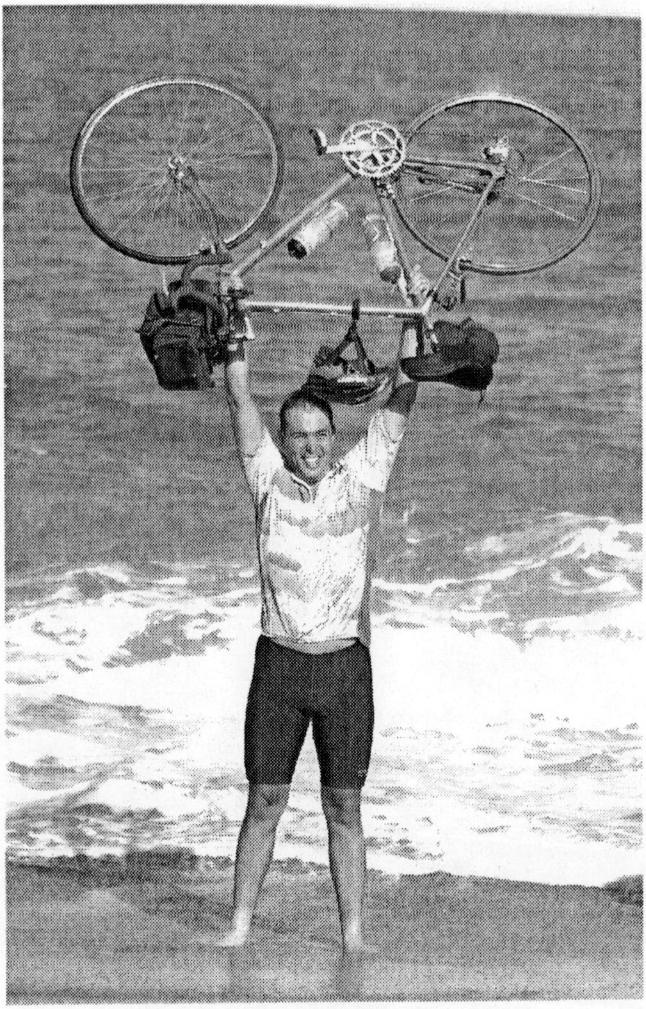

In conclusion:

"Whether you think you can or you think you can't, you're right."

For me, this was an incredible journey—incredible in every way. It was incredibly hard and incredibly rewarding. It helped bring clarity to my life. To this day, I tell people it was like a terrific movie I went to see, or a great book I read, or a dream I had. It didn't seem possible that I had done what I did. We faced a lot of adversity, and we had to dig very deep to work through it each day. It was the most physically and emotionally demanding thing I've ever done. By the time we ended our fundraising efforts, we had raised nearly $44,000.

I will always consider this to be one of the top accomplishments of my life. I feel as though I can do anything now. More than ever, I realize the importance and the power of the human spirit and the right attitude. Dr. Petrelli and I discussed this at the reception, and he told me that it's the same with people diagnosed with cancer: They need to resolve that they are going to beat it.

I am more prepared than ever for whatever life has in store for me. The ride enhanced my life, and I realized during that swim in the Atlantic that I would never be quite the same again. The unique bond I have with J.P., Ray, Larry, and Tim will be long lasting. We were, and are, a team.

Someone once told me the top three things that people say they wish they had accomplished at the conclusion of their lives. I view them as a sort of test for the quality of my life, and I understand them to be:

1. The ability to see the big picture *and* focus on what really matters in life each day.

2. The importance of being courageous each day.

3. The need to take the initiative to do something to make a difference.

The ride provided me the opportunity to accomplish all of these things, and I am grateful to our team for making it possible. Can I maintain it? I think the saying about the need to set your goals higher than you think you can reach, then reach them, is "right on". For me, the ride will always stand as a shining example of that principle.

The ride further opened my eyes to the common struggles people have that are out of their control. It helped me to realize how good life has been to me. It helped me to realize that fear is natural, but that allowing it to play too significant a role in anything will negatively impact outcomes and restrict the good that can come from within.

Rather than accommodating fear, as we all do at times, I accepted a challenge that was out of character for me and looked fear in the face—and I won. More good than I ever expected came from this ride, and I'll savor this victory and its many memories for the rest of my life.

Printed in the United States
56068LVS00005B/154-168